Momma Trauma:
Now What?

Finding HOPE when your child battles pornography or
other challenging issues

Steadfast strategies to stay centered on Jesus Christ

Karen Broadhead

Parent Support Specialist at Life Changing Services
and Founder and Director of *Mothers Who Know*

With excerpts from the "Parent's Appendix" of
Like Dragons Did They Fight

To my sons, *whose warrior hearts reminded me I had one too.*

Acknowledgements

Heavenly Father - *for having a winning plan for me, helping me find my warrior heart and success through His son, my Savior and Champion, Jesus Christ. For His confidence in me and showing me broken people can do amazing things, in a broken way. If I trust Him with all my heart, let go of "my" understanding and always remember Him...my messes are not mistakes, but miracles. Everything is God's work! He is the Creator, Director and Finisher. I'm just me, and nothing without Him.*

My husband - *for loving me in a way that made it safe for me to heal and grow. Without ever expecting more or pointing out less, he has always loved me for who I am and where I'm at. I adore you!*

Maurice Harker - *for hearing the call to create an inspired recovery program that brought us so much hope. A great friend and mentor, he allows me to create and has always been supportive of me and other warrior mothers.*

Connie - *for her vigilance as co-editor for this book, a consultant for MWK and the inspiring director of our mother's outreach team. You are my angel sister and forever best friend. Thank you for truly seeing me and believing in me. I am stronger, smarter, safer and braver with you by my side.*

April - *for formatting, layout, editing and assisting in all things MWK so beautifully. Your hard work, positive attitude and excitement about getting this book to print has kept us all going. You are evidence of God "sending someone to the rescue" to make weak things (like me/MWK) strong.*

Stacey - *for offering creative advice, adding finishing touches, getting us to print and coming up with the term "Momma Trauma." You have a heart without guile and an eloquence in expression that always invites the Spirit. Thank you for helping me feel smart. even when I don't feel like it.*

Jen - *for so willingly and speedily creating the illustrations for this book as well as being a fearless power mom on our mother's outreach team, on a mission to rescue the weary. You are my warrior sister in arms!*

Fellow Warrior Mothers Who Know - *for your courage to reach out and share in this book a little about where you are in your journey, so others can see themselves more clearly and truthfully in their journey. For courageously remembering why you fight and never giving up! You inspire me and help me to "stay by the tree."*

Author's Note

This book is a valuable resource for any mother in trauma no matter what issue she is facing with a child. You will read how I and other mothers fell into Momma Trauma because of a child's addiction to pornography. You may be experiencing hurt and pain related to a different struggle your child is battling, yet it is no less heart breaking. Momma Trauma is real and we all need support, training and healing.

Any mother feeling isolation or vulnerability needs a support system. I tried staying in isolation mode and I know many of you have too. In case you are just arriving in Momma Trauma, let me warn you isolation is a sure-fire way to get emotionally, spiritually and physically sick.

I hope the principles and training I share here will bring hope and healing to mothers in pain. But ultimately, WHERE CAN WE TURN FOR PEACE? WHERE IS OUR SOLACE? (LDS Hymns #129) Who can show us the best way to support our child? Who can assist us to know how to manage how much we care, love and desire to rescue our wounded child? Who can tell us what to do with our fear when we realize this isn't going to be a quick and easy fix? There is only ONE source for the healing and the hope we need: Jesus Christ, our merciful Redeemer – HE IS THE ONLY ONE!

Please join with me in taking one purposeful step at a time away from darkness and hurt towards light and hope. As warrior moms we can face the storms together with confidence, faith and courage as we support and love our children through any battle they may face.

Together in the fight!

Karen Broadhead

Foreword

by Maurice Harker, CMHC, Founder and Director
of Life Changing Services

I would like you to meet Karen Broadhead. She has become a dear friend to me and a vital part of the efforts we make at Life Changing Services to provide quality services to you and your loved ones.

I met Karen almost 10 years ago. She was, like you, a regular mom who loved her children, was trying to get it right but felt overwhelmed and less competent than she wanted. The daunting task of raising children in this lone and dreary world brought her a fear and concern that is familiar to you all.

She asked if she could help. We discussed computer work, filing and financial needs of the company, but each brought discord to her face. I then realized something I had not paid close enough attention to at the time. I realized she wasn't the only mother that was in pain. I was not able to be there for the mothers in a sufficiently meaningful way, so I asked her if she would just check in with the moms of sons in our programs and be a support to them.

Not only did Karen courageously start calling women she had never met before, but she also showed an incredible knack for helping soothe and comfort these ladies. Being anxious to serve and serve well, she was not satisfied with just comforting. She proceeded to work hard to discover and practice teaching principles and ideas to give mothers accurate interventions for their loved ones. She created a place for mothers to come together and provide unity and instruction for each other on how to handle difficult circumstances in their homes. She gave this organization the name *Mothers Who Know.*

Karen has stretched her comfort zone by not only gaining excellent teaching skills but also excellent leadership skills. She has developed a team of amazingly powerful moms who work together to provide all of us with audio trainings and videos that bring education, insight and hope to individuals and families all over the world. With her work, she has brought together and served thousands of mothers. And recently, she has helped create a service directly for fathers called *Fathers Who Fight.*

In addition to all that is listed above, Karen has become a vital friend and consultant for me. Karen brings with her a combination of strength and warmth that influences my ability to serve others. She has wisdom and courage when she shares her thoughts and ideas on how to improve our ability to serve. She brings an uplifting power to all meetings so everyone around her feels smarter, stronger and empowered to fulfill their stewardships. We lovingly refer to her as the mother of Life Changing Services.

I want you to meet my friend, Karen. I invite you to read what she has to say. She and her amazing team have worked very hard to provide this book for you. It is built upon a deep love for you and your loved ones as well as both spiritual and scientific accuracy. Please invite the spirit of personal revelation as you read and I am confident you will gain comfort, strength and insight for your stewardships.

Your Eternal Servant,

Maurice Harker

*"For God hath not given us the spirit of fear; but of **power**, and of **love**, and of a **sound mind**."*

-2 Timothy 1:7

Introduction

You just found out your son or daughter has an addiction to pornography, and you are in tears. Your child is in chains with a gaping wound like you have never seen before and you have no frame of reference or training on how to handle this. You need help! You need answers! You need to know what to do to help your fallen child. Everything in you wants to run for help, but you can't. Where would you go?

Your child has the kind of addiction that a mother must hide in order to protect them from even more danger and pain. If anyone were to find out your child was addicted to pornography, it would ruin them and affect their future. If anyone knew your child had an addiction to pornography, what would they think of you and your parenting?

No one can find out.

So, even though you feel like a death has taken place and you are in such great trauma, you have to show up in your life like nothing is happening at your house. You are feeling like you can hardly breathe with the weight of this shaming secret your son or daughter has kept from you, and now you must also carry it.

You are isolated and alone.

You become a policewoman, consumed with controlling the situation and frantic about making sure there are no more "slips" (hereafter called lost battles). You are hyper-vigilant about noticing everything and anything your child is doing so you can be there to protect them. You sleep in their room, stand by the shower door, monitor how much time they are alone and wonder how to manage yourself and all the stewardships you have with other children and activities that are part of your life.

You are exhausted and numb.

You are a woman who cries a lot and you want to scream when you see acquaintances out in public who ask you, as they always have, "How's it going?" with optimistic smiles on their well-meaning faces. You say the only thing you can say, "Good, how about you?" But deep down you want

1

to yell and say, "How's it going??? Well, it's going and gone my
friend! Over the fence and into the stratosphere!! I am in a mess of such
proportion that it can't be described! I am disgusted, tired, exhausted,
angry, depressed, lonely, hurt, betrayed and completely lost...how about
you?"

You are angry and hurt.

You know you should be turning to God and finding your faith. You are
going to do it tomorrow and then tomorrow comes and goes. You just
can't seem to approach God and you can't figure out if it's because you are
angry at Him or know that He must be angry and disappointed in you.
How could you let such a horrible thing happen to a child He trusted you
to teach correctly and keep safe? Feeling hollow and stuck, there
are endless questions about how you got here and why.

You are embarrassed and ashamed.

You keep wondering how this happened. You were doing all the right
things, checking all the "this is the gospel in action" boxes. "Aren't there
promises associated with obedience and faithfulness? Isn't the Spirit
supposed to warn me of danger when I need it? Where was God and
where is He now? I don't deserve this and neither does my child." So, you
decide the best thing to do is keep walls up all around you because now,
even in an arena where you were supposed to be safe and expect help,
you are hurt and alone. It just doesn't make sense.

You are losing your faith and confidence.

Your son or daughter needs help and that is your focus. But you need help
too. You are wounded at a level you have never experienced before. You
are withdrawn and feel like you might lose your mind. You know your
heart is broken because it physically hurts and sometimes you are having
difficulty breathing. You are wounded and need healing. You are all alone
with nowhere safe to turn.

You are in Momma Trauma.

Momma Trauma is real and difficult to avoid in a day where we are literally parenting our children in a war zone against the adversary! Our enemy, Satan, is determined in his destructive cause to take us out of our purpose and thwart God's plan for each of us. Satan's greatest filthy lie is pornography. Even the best of our youth has fallen and continue to sustain severe wounds. Some of our noblest warriors (our youth) have fallen prey and become prisoners of war. Our children are all warriors in this war against the adversary.

When you have a child in addiction you can experience so much shame, go through a mountain of negative emotions and feel like you have completely lost your footing and sense of direction. This sense of powerlessness can crack your internal compass and leave you in a place with far more questions than answers, feeling a complete loss of hope. What is a mother who is experiencing Momma Trauma to do?

I was in that darkness and feel great empathy for mothers in their own version of the same. In writing this book, I am extending a safe and courageous hand to kindly invite you to consider LIGHT. You wouldn't be in the dark unless you believed it was a safer place to be. You are meant for light! You are meant to have peace and purpose. There is hope, healing and help for you and your loved one. You are a "Mother Who Knows." You are a warrior of light, ready to stand against the darkness of this world. I want to help you learn to fight and come out of the darkness and overcome those feelings of despair. There is free support and training to assist you *one step at a time*. *"For God hath not given us the spirit of fear; but of power, and of love, and of a sound mind"* (2 Timothy 1:7, KJV).

"I have been meaning to email you and give you an update on my son. He is headed to the ---------- mission in March. He is the most amazing young man! We have grown really close through this tough experience, and we are able to talk about a lot of things that we would never have been able to, if we had not gone through this experience. I am amazed at how Heavenly Father can take the most terrible, heartbreaking, or painful experiences and turn them for

our good; whether we bring them on ourselves or not. It is just another testimony of how He is not only all-loving but all-powerful. Nothing is beyond his ability to fix. He will not be stopped or hindered in any way when it comes to loving and helping His children.

I have also learned a deep and powerful lesson about Satan's power and the way that he works. I thought he had power over me, but it turns out that I am way more powerful than he is and so are my children and all of us. I can say, "Get lost Satan, I don't have to listen to you at all, you have no power over me because I am yoked with Jesus Christ, and you will never in a billion lifetimes beat Him!" I love the power of knowing that Satan has to leave and that he is probably sulking about it too! I'm so happy to know where the source of my depression or anger really comes from and how I can quickly and easily get out of it.

My son has become an inspiration to me and I have confidence that I can have a great relationship with my other son and my daughters because of all that I have learned in this program. I have a great love and respect for anyone who is struggling with this problem [pornography addiction] and I would be **proud** to know any man, woman, or young person who is dealing with this because they scare Satan and shake his world! Why else would he try so hard to take them down? That is so inspiring! I feel truly, mercifully, blessed! Thank you, Karen, for your great work!" (A very grateful Warrior Mom)

A Warrior's Mother: My Story

"They had been taught by their mothers, that if they did not doubt, God would deliver them" (Alma 56:47, *Book of Mormon*).

My Family - Under Attack:

I'll never forget the day my son came home from attending his second week in his Sons of Helaman group. He yelled, "Mom!" from our back entry. As he was not known to do that sort of thing, I worried something had gone wrong at group. When I came upon him he was bent over, visibly shaking with emotion, trying to compose himself enough to communicate something to me. I stood there waiting and wondering, not knowing whether to be worried or hopeful. Finally, he gave up and with more ferocity and emotion than I had ever seen, he put his hands on my shoulders and said, "Mom, I am not the enemy. I have an enemy and he's afraid of me. He knows I'm awesome. He's trying to take me out so I can't become the man I'm supposed to be. I'm not a pathetic loser! I'm not my enemy...he is! He's going down!!"

My son was learning to stand.

He was 16 at the time. We discovered his addiction to pornography at the age of 13 and were devastated to realize it had been going on for two years. We were afraid when we realized how far things had escalated and were shocked our noble, good son was in the bonds of addiction. The shame I felt as a mother was overwhelming. I was tormented with thoughts of blaming myself for his addiction. I had so much to learn about my son, myself and especially about the power of Jesus Christ.

I was beyond grateful to have found a program that would train my son to "win his battles" and eventually, win the war. I thought my role was to jump in with more intensity than ever and do all "I" could do to help him fight. My role would be getting completely involved and watching his every move. I can remember asking myself, "What can I do to make sure he doesn't ever do this again?" I worked really hard to insert my love, my discipline, my encouragement, my new boundaries for him, and my determination that "NO MATTER WHAT, I WILL SAVE THIS BOY!"

We were at war and I was going to make sure he won. I watched, prayed, bossed him around, checked on him all the time, made charts, developed rewards and consequences. Every time my son fell down in battle, I would beg him to stand back up and keep fighting. In my mind, I had to hoist his bruised body on my shoulders and swing his sword (the one I had just sharpened) at every temptation in order to ensure his victory.

My Awakening:

I was the mother of a warrior who was fighting valiantly for his life, but because of my lack of knowledge and my great fear of failure, I found it impossible to trust his efforts. It had been devastating to find out my son was in the bonds of addiction. It was debilitating to finally realize I was powerless to heal him no matter how much I tried. I wondered where God was and why he wasn't helping us. My belief in the power of the Savior to heal was affected.

I started writing letters to God, one of the techniques my son had learned in the Sons of Helaman program. I wrote down my concerns, fears and questions about how to help my son. When an idea would fill me with peace, I wrote down the answer God was whispering. In doing so, I learned something in the spirit: my son already had a Savior, and it wasn't me. It is God's job, His work and glory to *save*, not mine.
I was making it difficult for God to do His work with my son. I was losing hope and confidence in myself AND my son. I began to realize as a "mother who knows," I too had an enemy who was trying to take me out and decrease my confidence. I needed the Savior to save my son and I needed Him to save me from my false thinking and broken heart. I realized I had to get out of the way and start asking how I could help support God in His work with my son.

The Stand:

I approached Maurice Harker, the director of the Sons of Helaman program, in tears which were evidence of my overwhelmed and heavy heart. I asked him if I could do anything to help because my "mother energy" was in overdrive and I needed to do something. He put me straight to work on quality control issues in the office, but I was terrified to talk to other mothers who had a son in the program. When I did, I found they were either in such a place of shame and pain they didn't know how to talk about their son's addiction OR they were so happy to have someone to talk to, they would go to town and spill it all. The isolation we were all feeling was feeding our shame and pain. I was not the only one who was exhausted...everyone was going through the same thing and life looked sad and scary at their house too. There were other mothers who knew exactly what I was going through!

With Maurice's approval, *Mothers Who Know* (MWK) was created. MWK is a free, weekly, powerful, online support group for mothers/parents all over the country.

The Victory:

Being supportive of my warrior looked a lot different than I had thought; it started with my own healing...not with healing my son. It became clear that the best way to support my noble son was to let him see his mother did not doubt God's power to deliver him (Alma 56:47). To truly be magnified as a mother, I needed to be filled with God's love and partake of the grace he freely offered. To me, this meant "staying by the tree" of life at all times where God's love could change me.

No matter how long it took my son to make it to the tree, I had to stay put and beckon from where I was. I cheered, testified of the Lord's power and pointed him to his Captain and Champion, Jesus Christ when my son was in a battle. I prayed, believed, handed him water bottles, helped him shine up his armor, made sure he was wearing his helmet and then sent him into battle with his God. I praised him for protecting me, manning up and fighting for himself, for me and for his future wife and family.

I was on the front lines of faith in my son's battle, reminding him I could do some things for him, but ultimately, God could do all things for him. "Go find God - you can trust Him! He will teach you how to fight, He will teach you how to win, He will change your desires, He will help you carry your burden."

I feel so privileged to be the mother of my warrior son and to have gone on this journey with him. After years of struggle, fully armed with the tools he acquired in the Sons of Helaman program and with a testimony of His Savior, my son went on to serve an honorable LDS mission. He married a wonderful woman in the Salt Lake Temple and started a family. He feels extremely blessed to have been trained with tools to combat this addiction throughout his life and even more grateful to have a personal testimony of where healing comes from and how this happened for him.

It is wonderful, from a mother's perspective, to know he has this training and his testimony. It gives me great comfort to know he has the tools for success to call upon and to assist him to successfully journey through this life.

If you have a son or daughter struggling with addiction or other challenging issues, please know there is always hope. Align yourself with the Savior and focus on fighting your own battles. You will become a stronger, more confident, peaceful warrior mother even as your child heads out to war. In the end, because of our Lord and Savior Jesus Christ, both you and your child will win. *"Trust in the Lord with all thine heart; and lean not unto thine own understanding. In all thy ways acknowledge him, and he shall direct thy paths"* (Proverbs 3:5-6, KJV).

Cries for Help
(names withheld to protect privacy)
What Can I Do to Help My Son or Daughter?

"I am a mother of one daughter (who is married) and five sons ages 12-22. I have recently discovered that all five of my sons are struggling with pornography addiction, including the oldest who is a recent Returned Missionary and newlywed. My emotions have been all over the place, and I'm trying to decide where to start! My heart has been tormented the last two weeks since becoming aware that not just one or two, but ALL five of my boys have this addiction. I have done some serious soul searching the past few weeks. I have been made aware that this is one of the main reasons I am on the earth at this time and why all of these boys were sent to me. Because I am a Warrior Mama! I don't want to mess this up!"

"I know we are all fighting for our children. How do we fight for ourselves? Our situation is as unique as anyone's. My son was arrested a month ago. We have been to court and lawyers. He is 16. Everyone in our community and ward knows what happened. I have had to quit my job and stay home with him. We do homebound school and home seminary. I have had a few people reach out to me and a very, very negative reaction from someone in our Relief Society presidency. My own anxieties are terrible. I don't want to go to church. I do and I smile and do my calling and everything, then go hide in the mother's room and cry. My question is: How do we face these things? I'm trying so hard to be strong. My testimony is very strong but I know church is not always safe. My life is crazy! I would appreciate any advice."

"My son has a pornography/masturbation problem. He has a strong testimony but has not been able to take the sacrament for over a year! He started out talking to the bishop once a week, but it slowly became longer and longer between times. Now he hasn't seen him in months. He doesn't like to talk about it with me, and my husband thinks it will just go away. He

is 16 1/2 and I don't see how anything is going to change since nothing we have done thus far has helped. Is there any help for him? Can you just help me to know what I should be doing - pressing the issue of counseling or letting it alone? I am very non-judgmental about his situation. I fear for his future and feel like there is no one to talk to about it. Everyone I can talk to seems to treat it so lightly. My nephew attended your program [Sons of Helaman] and it helped him to get on his mission, but I don't want to talk to my sister because I don't want to break a confidence with my son. Thank you for anything you can help me with."

"This is about my 16-year-old daughter. She expressed to me just this past summer that she has been struggling with attraction to the same sex. She definitely is attracted to boys but she is feeling this pull toward girls as well. This is something she has told me she has felt for several years but was always afraid to tell me. I am SO grateful that she has felt safe enough to come to me and lean on me with this trial. After the initial shock and trying not to be devastated that she is having to deal with this and may have to deal with this struggle for the rest of her life.

She and I have talked about the Plan of Happiness. She understands, I think, that this is a trial in her life and that her struggle isn't a sin, but only if she were to act on it. She has a tremendous testimony. I am beyond impressed with her desire to serve the Lord and be obedient. But I also know that at 16 (almost 17) she will have tremendous trials within this realm yet. She desires to serve a mission and understands and supports the guidelines of the Church.

I need help!! Is there ANYWHERE online or otherwise that can be a source of support for her? She feels isolated from the youth in the ward. Mainly, I think because of her struggles and feeling different. Anything you think can give her ongoing support and help would be greatly appreciated!

As an aside, I never in a million years thought I would be having to address these kinds of things with my kids at this age - maybe drinking or sex or drugs, but not this. This is the way the adversary is attacking our children - makes me sad."

"I have two sons in the program, almost 16 and 18 ½. My 16-year old still loses an occasional battle, but is implementing the strategies and is open

with me about things. I'm careful, but we do talk regularly about things related to all of this, including specific tools, etc. I feel good about his progress, especially because I feel like he is using the Atonement in his life...yay!!!

My 18-year old is not progressing at all. He has struggled with this problem for several years, since he was a child, really (well, both of them for that matter). He can't make it more than a couple of days without losing a battle. He hasn't blessed the sacrament in over a year, yet he attends Sacrament meeting with us (and all of church) every week and sits through the Sacrament service, not partaking himself, as agreed upon with the bishop. I am truly grateful and amazed at his ability to even do this, as he is someone who is often very sensitive to what others think of him. I imagine this is very hard for him. Yet, it is not enough to motivate him to do better. He does not apply what he is learning in class and will talk about stuff if I ask, but we don't get far because he just seems to not want to deal with it. I have stopped asking him about things as frequently. Now maybe once a week if that.

What am I missing? I keep hearing things need to be transparent, but I'm worried that I won't do it right, or that my involvement will make things worse. (I have a tendency to micro-manage, though I'm aware of it and working hard not to do it.) Any thoughts? My most HUGE concern is that I feel that he has not found the Savior in a real way. He has not learned to apply the Atonement. I have discussed this with him several times, and even begged him to just ask Him for help, but I don't think he has done even that. I don't understand why he won't include the Savior. He is SUCH a good kid (like you hear all the time). Everyone loves him, he has a lot of friends, he is good and kind and every adult's favorite. It's almost like he has taken this part of his life and compartmentalized it so that he doesn't have to think about it or feel bad about it or deal with it. Sorry to be so lengthy. I just don't know what to do."

"I am writing to you because I need some reassurance. My son is 15 and has been in a therapy program since last October. He joined Sons of Helaman a couple of months ago. I felt like he was doing really well until recently he has been struggling. My anxiety has gone through the roof! I find myself trying to hold on tight to him and question everything he is doing! This, of course, backfires on me in a big way and he gets angry. He told me today that he has been struggling to feel God's love for him, which breaks my heart because he is a very spiritual boy. Can you enlighten me?"

"My son viewed pornography about a year ago and met with the bishop and then he has viewed it again. He is meeting with the bishop again. His dad and I are divorced so he isn't with me all the time. I communicate fairly well with his dad. I know that he is able to read the scriptures at my house but I'm not sure what he is able to do at his dad's. How can I teach my son self-control so he is not tempted to look at it?"

"Five months ago we found out our son was addicted to porn and has acted out on it. To say I am devastated is beyond words. My heart is completely shattered and my anger is high. What would you recommend would be the best way to start healing? I feel like my world is shattered beyond repair and I will never come out of this strong. I have a lot of anger towards my son and have blamed myself, wondering if I could have done more to prevent this. Any advice on steps to take for my healing would be incredibly appreciated.
Sincerely,
A devastated and heartbroken mom"

"My son, who turned 39 this year, is wonderful. He has 4 beautiful children, a fabulous wife and is very successful financially. And he is an addict. It started with sexual abuse at age 6 of which I was unaware until he told us in his 20's after viewing porn for 14 years. I had to seek help for the enraged feelings I had for the perpetrators and he has been in counseling for many years himself. He is still an addict. He reaches out to both me and my husband but has lapses that cross boundaries and he has to leave his home, wife and kids for a while. I pray every day for him. My heart aches for all he has been through and the fact that we, his parents, did NOT protect him. I struggle with guilt every time he struggles. So, how can I help him? I know he knows we love him and always will. I love his wonderful wife and our beautiful grandchildren. I want to see him CONQUER THIS. I feel like an armchair quarterback, only cheering him on, but NOT doing anything really. He can do this, he is exceptionally brilliant, a spiritual giant, a good husband and father. What more can I do?"

"I am searching for help for my two sons, ages 16 and 14. Their problems began with an addiction to pornography, which I became aware of a few years ago. I tried fighting the problem by putting restrictions on the computer, but my older son only saw that as a challenge and successfully defeated the restrictions. I eventually decided we could not have a computer in the house and got rid of it. Then my husband decided they needed smartphones. I tried putting restrictions on the smartphones, but those restrictions were successfully defeated as well, so I got rid of the smartphones in favor of flip phones. The boys hate the flip phones and have resorted several times to stealing others' smartphones or shoplifting technology products from Walmart and using apps over Wi-Fi to get what they want. I got a router for home with filtering capabilities which has helped some, but there is still the library where devices that log into their free Wi-Fi can be unfiltered. Needless to say, they spend a lot of time at the library. I share all this in hopes you can offer me some options as I feel just about out of them."

"I have four boys, and my oldest got exposed to pornography while sitting in a classroom at ___ High School one day while another student was viewing it on his phone in class. Ta Da! Well, since that time, my oldest, who is 25, will have episodes of viewing it. I don't feel he is an addict, but when his dopamine levels go south, that is when he looks at it. It is off and on, kind of like a social drinker. The ball still rolls down. My son who is 18, and on a mission, was exposed from his brother and was able to break the cycle. But, my concern is when he returns and adjusts back to real life, it will return. Now I have the two younger boys at home. They are turning 11 and 12, and I know sexuality needs to be discussed and I want to do this right."

"I just found out that my 10-year-old son has been looking at pornography for the last month. My world is crashing down, and I am almost suicidal at this news. I feel guilt and shame and anger. Where do I go? Who do I talk to?"

Mothers Who Know

Specializing in supporting mothers in trauma

Motto: Stay by the Tree

Scripture: *"For God hath not given us the spirit of fear; but of power, and of love, and of a sound mind"* (2 Timothy 1:7).

Hello fellow parent! I am Karen Broadhead, a warrior for Jesus Christ and a Mother Who Knows. If you are feeling like you are in a mess, I say with confidence...you are not alone, there are thousands of other parents who can relate to the pain you are feeling and are searching for healing for their child too. After 10 years of experience with parents, and under the tutelage of Maurice Harker, I hope to share some vital things I have learned over the years to be of consistent value to parents, especially mothers.

I desire to give all the credit to the Lord. He is the best tutor and mentor. Anything I say or do which speaks truth or inspires is because He is the author of it. I truly am a very broken person with many flaws seeking to do amazing things in a very broken way because heaven is helping me (and all of us). I have come to learn the Holy Ghost is truly our teacher. As we learn to listen with the Spirit, we can discern those things that will be right for OUR family and OUR situation, unique to each of us. Our stories may all be a little different, but we can definitely learn from each other and will find in many ways, our stories really are the same - we are all fighting the same enemy and we all seek to win with the Lord's help.

There is so much to learn and understand when you discover complicated issues in your family. It is easy to feel like you just don't know what you are doing. As parents in a panic to find resources and recovery for our child, we rarely consider we also have a need for recovery from the trauma caused by the situation and the many wounds we sustain as our loved ones fight their battles to win.

Mothers Who Know was started with the goal to bring mothers/parents out of the darkness of despair and fear and into the light of hope. We facilitate a weekly online group where mothers across the country can join in support of each other, as well as come to learn tools and principles to best support their son or daughter. (We also have a once a month group called *Fathers Who Fight™*). These groups provide free education in a webinar classroom format to empower you to stand strong against the opposition of our day. We shine light on the tactics used by the adversary to discourage women and threaten families. (Note: *Mothers Who Know* and *Fathers Who Fight* are open to everyone. You do not need to have a child in one of our addiction recovery programs to participate.)

Our mission in *Mothers Who Know* is to encourage all to find the strength they need through the Atonement of our Savior, Jesus Christ. We specialize in supporting mothers whose son or daughter is dealing with an addiction, patterns of unwanted behavior or any issue that requires therapeutic intervention.

Satan knows how dangerous women standing in the truth of their divine identity and purpose are. He will do all in his power to confuse us about our identity and purpose. He knows he can't take us out; we are far too strong for that. But he can make us cry, doubt, fear or lose our confidence. He can take away our voice and courage, until we are numb and confused. He knows he can more easily accomplish his destructive mission of misery if *good women are asleep with their eyes open* (meaning you may look awake and present, but on the inside, you are full of turmoil, numbness, pain, confusion, hurt, and betrayal). Often, we are convinced that staying in isolation or in a numb state is the only way to handle our pain and maintain sanity. We are going through the motions, but have a loss of hope, drive or spirituality. Those who are isolated and stay in the dark get very sick and wounded in the war.

Two empowering things happened for my son when he got involved in Sons of Helaman. First, he came out of isolation and realized he was not the only good person struggling. Second, he could see and feel increased light and hope in his battle. He could see evidence the training worked as he applied it for himself. He also watched and gained strength from others who had gone before him. He gained strength through seeing their successes as they were applying their training.

Simply put, my son needed support and training. What I have come to realize, is those who are supporting a loved one also need support and training.

My son needed a place where he was focused on the war he was fighting and could realize he has a real enemy determined to destroy his dreams and hopes for the future. He needed to know he was not in this fight alone. Others were winning...and with training and discipline, SO COULD HE. Most importantly, he needed to take all the shame he had built up over years of losing battles and defining himself falsely because of it, and focus all this shame and anger on to the real enemy. There was great power when my son could stop fighting with himself; thinking he was his own worst enemy, and start protecting himself at many levels...spiritually, physically and emotionally from the real enemy. Parents need to learn to do the same.

One way we as parents can protect ourselves spiritually, is to *wake up* and realize we are at war and it is far more personal than we think. It changed my life to learn the same things my son was learning and apply them to my own personal battles with self-mastery. It was exciting and liberating to reclaim my own identity and purpose and stand confidently with a whole new perspective about what was going on around me and inside of me. I had never recognized that the war we fight is in our minds and hearts.

I AM THE CRUSHER!
Satan is just a *bruiser*.

When I realized what was happening and that I had power to change and a Savior who was right there to assist me, it was AMAZING!!! My life changed because I recognized my enemy and began to gain knowledge and insight into how to discern and detect the real enemy. But most empowering was to learn "I was the CRUSHER!!" I could now fight back.

Instead of being on the defense, trying to avoid being tricked by Satan and pulled onto his "smoke and mirrors" battle field...I began to recognize I could strategically *plan, prepare and practice* in an offensive way. It was like saying; "Ok Lucifer, I can see you and I know we are going to battle today and every day because you, like the Lamanites in the *Book of Mormon* will never stop trying to kill the Nephites...so I invite you to meet me on my battlefield where I have home court advantage. I refuse to fight you on your terms, on your field, or in your sick way." I, like my hero Captain Moroni, have put on the kind of preparation and armor spoken of in Alma 43:18-19, 21:

> *"And it came to pass that [Karen] met [Satan] in the borders of [her mind and heart], and [her] people were armed with swords, and with cimeters and all manner of weapons of war.*
>
> *And when the armies of [Satan] saw that [Karen and her family], or that [Karen], had prepared [her] people with breastplates and with arm-shields, yea, and also shields to defend their heads, and also they were dressed with thick clothing...—*
>
> *therefore, they were exceedingly afraid."*

Can you see in your own life how easy it is to get in a fog and forget to dress in protective armor - to pray, read the scriptures, go to the temple, attend church to renew your promises of why you fight? I can! It became blaringly obvious to me how hard Satan worked to weaken me by distracting me and deceiving me away from the simple things I am to do each day to protect myself. My morning motto is "armor up!" I refuse to show up to battle against a 7000-year-old military and psychological genius who is sneaky and mean without my full armor every day. I have to remind myself of this daily. I now have personal battle strategies to maintain the strength of my armor and battle plans, daily and often. I have learned Satan is always walking about like a lion, watching me to see where my weaknesses are and how he can devour me (1 Peter 5:8).

Captain Moroni is an amazing example of what it takes to win battles against an enemy who will never stop trying to have power over you, put you in bondage as a prisoner of war or kill you. He prepared ahead of time for the attack in astonishingly cool ways, and so must we.

> *"For behold, [Satan's] designs were to stir up [his army] to anger against the [Broadheads]; this he did that he might usurp great power over them, and also that he might gain power over the [Broadheads] by bringing them into bondage.*

17

And now the design of the [Broadheads] was to support their lands, and their houses, and their wives, and their children, that they might preserve them from the hands of their enemies, and also that they might preserve their rights and their privileges, yea, and also their liberty, that they might worship God according to their desires [in spirit and in truth]" (Alma 43:8-9).

Just like Captain Moroni planned and instructed the people he loved to wear cool armor that frightens the enemy, use strategic tactics and make detailed battle plans, we as parents must do the same. It's time we all *wake up the warrior we have always been and remember why we fight and why we don't give up!* We have already proven we know how to fight against Satan; the fact that we are here proves we have fought a battle against him before AND WON! We bravely fight out of loyalty, love and support of our Father in Heaven and all He offers to us and has planned for us. We truly want to be like Him. We fight for the great cause of freedom our Savior and Champion, Jesus Christ, claimed for us. We stand and fight with purpose and confidence because of Him. He is "the way" (John 14:6) to victory. Without Him we are utterly lost. Our battle cry should be something like: "We believe in Christ's promises and the miracles he has performed for us – 'be strong in the Lord, *and in the power of his might!'"* (Ephesians 6:10). As parents we can choose to *wake up* and then do what it takes to *stay awake!*

Healing, hope and a powerful connection to his divine nobility as a son of God propelled my son to regain hope and confidence in the great future he had, despite his mistakes, because he was awesome! When he could detect Satan's lies about his identity, recognize the lie that the Atonement was out of his reach and see Satan's subtle, yet debilitating tactics, he found the confidence to stand! Satan knows that no matter how much knowledge, training, truth and skill a person has - if he is fighting himself, feeling shame, lacking confidence or remaining in emotional pain, it makes it easier to work his weapons against him and keep him trapped where he is.

I have noticed from personal experience as a mother, trainer and *Mothers Who Know* facilitator, that as parents, we too need to recognize Satan's lies, face our emotional pain and be more aware of the war we face and our vital role in it. It is hard to stand and fight with the kind of courage it takes to defend and protect our families from the great onslaught of opposition unless we can wake up the warrior within ourselves and remember who we have always been. We too must have some serious skills at fighting the enemy or we won't be able to be the parents we were meant to be in this great and last day! It can feel overwhelming and even debilitating as we try to do so, if we don't access the same powerful training our sons and daughters are receiving in the programs at Life Changing Services. Join in the strength and support of *Mothers Who Know* and our newest support and training group *Fathers Who Fight*. Keep reading for advice and basic training skills for parents. (We go more in-depth in our classes and groups.)

You can read more about *Mothers Who Know* and its various classes here: www.lifechangingservices.org/motherswhoknow. Sons of Helaman (addiction recovery for young men), *Daughters of Light* (addiction recovery for young women and women of all ages) or *Eternal Warriors* (self-mastery/addiction prevention for youth, adults or families) are also offered through Life Changing Services at www.lifechangingservices.org.

Before I begin, I want to emphasize: There is only one thing worse than finding out your child has an addiction to pornography and/or masturbation...and that's not finding out. Now let's get started...

Ways to Overcome Momma Trauma
How to find strength, peace, comfort and joy

#1 - Build a Firm Foundation
As a parent, first make sure you are anchored deeply in the true foundation.

At the risk of sounding insensitive, I say, "Welcome to the storm, Warrior Parent."

I have a testimony of Helaman 5:12:

"And now, my sons, remember, remember that it is upon the rock of our Redeemer, who is Christ, the Son of God, that ye must build your foundation; that when the devil shall send forth his mighty winds, yea, his shafts in the whirlwind, yea, when all his hail and his mighty storm shall beat upon you, it shall have no power over you to drag you down to the gulf of misery and endless wo, because of the rock upon which ye are built, which is a sure foundation, a foundation whereon if men build they cannot fall."

If we are working on our foundation in Christ as parents, no matter how scary the storms are and how relentlessly they seem to beat upon us, we can still stand and fight, even lean into raging storms. When we have figured out who Christ, the Son of God, is to us personally and for our families, we don't have to fear all the fiery darts of the adversary; they will have no power over us to drag us *"down to the eternal gulf of misery and woe"* (2 Nephi 1:13). Satan is no match for the Savior in this great spiritual battle we fight. We will not fall if we are anchored in Him as we are tested in storms of opposition. *We know where we stand, why we don't move and by what source we maintain our courage!*

This gives great meaning to D&C 87:8, *"stand ye in holy places, and be not moved, until the day of the Lord come."*

The safest place to stand in battle is with and for our Savior

and Champion Jesus Christ. Through the grace of our Savior Jesus Christ, we will win! As women and daughters, we are God's secret weapon. Even in our relentless weakness, we are fierce protectors. We fight and bear pain with those who are wounded in a way no one else can. Our ability to believe and have hope in darkness and hold on until the light comes makes us formidable targets in this war.

As women, we know we are not the Savior in this war, but rather "atmosphere angels" who can change the very tide of the battle. We know where our power and strength come from. We are safe, strong, peaceful and protective warriors. We rely on the Savior to help us fight our battles and protect our families.

*"**With God Nothing is Impossible**: There's so much I would love to share with mothers. It's been about seven years since I learned about my sons' involvement in pornography, and there were some very rough days in those years. The thing I want most to say is there IS hope. You can hope for days when your heart doesn't ache all day, wondering if your son will be okay. There were days when I woke up so angry at satan that I could have sworn. I was SO angry that he had attacked my pure, sweet boys. I was SO angry that he had destroyed my husband and my marriage. But you need to know that I am at peace now. I still know that each day, I am in hand-to-hand combat with satan (I purposely don't capitalize his name - I don't think he deserves that honor), and I fight with all my might. Yes, some days I get a little weary of it - but then I remember Moroni, and Mormon, and how they kept fighting to the very end - and I know I can keep going too.*

The worst thing I did when my boys were first working through the Sons of Helaman program was to worry. I worried if they were still viewing. I worried if I needed to check up on them. All they saw was my worried face all the time. I wish I had just let it go. My job was to connect them to Maurice - and I wish at that point I had just been their cheerleader from then on. That is what I try to be now. I keep telling them how wonderful and amazing they are (because you know they truly are; if satan attacked them, he knew of their great potential and wants to thwart it!) and I try to live the best life I can so I'm always able to say what they need to hear. I always want them to see in me the joy the gospel brings, and for them to find hope in my love for them.

Keep loving them! They need our love more than anything else we can give them - love, and a good example of trusting in God. Because I have learned that truly, with God, nothing is impossible." (A Warrior Mother)

#2 - Know Your Enemy
It is vital to our success to have an understanding and healthy respect for (but not fear of) Satan who sends his mighty storms to beat upon and inside us and our families.

The fight is very personal because Satan's attacks are very personal.

He often attacks us through various negative thoughts in our heads, making us feel like we are awful parents, or have done something wrong, or didn't do something right or basically messed up our kids. However, we must realize not every voice in our head is a trusted voice. He is called the most subtle beast in the field (Moses 4:5, *Pearl of Great Price*) because he has figured out a way to attack us at a personal level, completely unnoticed.

The father of all lies uses our natural tendencies and chemical makeup to put us to sleep while our eyes are open - and slowly wraps us in his chains. The most maddening part is unless we are well trained and watchful, he can even convince us to think there is something fundamentally wrong with us, or we have no self-control or we actually chose the chains that bind us. What a sick, rude bully, right?!

This is war. We are in a spiritual war. If you are a parent and reading this you are likely here because you have some serious wounds at your house and your child is in essence, a prisoner of war.

Wounds sustained in a spiritual war can be terrifying to covenant keeping people who thought they were checking all the right boxes to protect their families. It can affect our faith, hope, courage and cause great confusion...leading to an inability to make smart decisions.

> BUT, BEHOLD, IT MATTERETH NOT WE TRUST *God* WILL DELIVER US, NOTWITHSTANDING THE WEAKNESS OF OUR ARMIES, YEA AND DELIVER US OUT OF THE HANDS OF OUR ENEMIES!
>
> THE *Lord* HAS SUPPORTED THEM, YEA AND KEPT THEM FROM FALLING — **not one** SOUL HAS BEEN **slain** BUT BEHOLD, THEY HAVE RECEIVED MANY **wounds.**
>
> ALMA 58:37-40

We are in shock at the wounds of our child and their exposure to the atrocities of this war. We feel *ambushed* and often unprepared for battles at such an intense level. We wonder how we missed something so severe which brings with it such far reaching consequences for our loved one and for us. It becomes obvious our loved one is under attack. If we are going to successfully get through this experience and be of the most value to our son or daughter, we must realize we are under attack as well.

You have probably already noticed it. It shows up as tormenting thoughts and feelings that are not edifying, to say the least. Most of these attacks will be about your abilities as a parent, about trying to make sense of where it all went wrong, about who is to blame. You begin to fear what this means for the future and how you or your loved one will be affected by it. You might be thinking awful things you would never want anyone to hear about your loved one. You might feel like quitting or giving up because you are convinced your family would be better off without you. You might even be withdrawing from your Father in Heaven because you are convinced He is disappointed in you for allowing this to happen to His child on your watch.

THESE ARE ALL SATANIC INSPIRED LIES!!!

You have only 1 ENEMY

If you are blaming yourself or others, thinking all is lost and living in a place of despair, I invite you to become more aware of the enemy of your soul and what his motives are with you and your family. If your child is in our recovery groups, they are being taught they are NOT their own worst enemy, rather they have an enemy and he is trying to take them out because he is afraid of them! The same is true of parents, perhaps even more so.

The enemy can keep us as parents from the power that comes from purposeful connections with our families and others who can help us. He knows that together we achieve more and there is great strength in numbers. His tactics are:

- DON'T ASK FOR HELP/SILENCE – Satan convinces us we need to help ourselves to save face or not appear weak.
- ISOLATION – Satan can make us believe we are all alone, no one is as messed up as we are, we don't fit in, we don't have a team that understands, no one cares and we should keep secrets and tell lies to protect the dark corner we are backed into.
- SHAME – He makes us think we should have known better or done better. When others find out what is going on in our house, they will know how bad we are. He will make you think things like, "You should hide quickly, there's something fundamentally wrong with you, people will reject you and no longer accept you or want you."
- CONTENTION – Satan is the father of all lies and loves contention. He will make you think things like, "You don't match your team, you are better than they are, they are too broken for you to be with, you didn't ask for this or sign up for this pain and confusion, you need to just give them an ultimatum. If they really loved you they would _____."

Again, these are all Satan's LIES! His way of endless torment causes us increased discomfort, anxiety and depression, distracting us away from our true source of healing - the Savior Jesus Christ.

Stay focused on your foundation in Christ (see #1). Remember the Savior and Champion of us all and how motivated He is to make sure you succeed. He has no doubt you are up to this journey and has great empathy for where you are and what you are feeling. This is your great opportunity to allow yourself to buckle in and have a front row seat at watching and experiencing how the power of the Atonement works in your life and in the life of your loved one.

So, I counsel you: Don't listen to Satan's lies. Don't allow him the satisfaction of tormenting you to the point of despair. Take this opportunity to be transformed and enlightened in your testimony of how unfailing our Heavenly Father's love is and how miraculous Christ, the Son of the Living God, is as you are schooled and carried by Him through this. Truly, His grace is sufficient for you and your child.

"All Healing Comes Through Christ: *All healing for us and our families comes through Christ and one of the biggest things to identify in order to do this is to recognize our real enemy and what he is doing to prevent our healing and our ability to find Christ and claim the power He offers us. No one notices Satan more than a woman who is in trauma. And believe me, I have been in trauma! The way Satan tormented me was relentless. But I learned that the opposite is true as well - no one notices Christ's power more than a woman who has learned how to find the Savior and access His power no matter what storms are in her life. I learned that I can cause waves of healing for others and fight my battles in the spirit. Nothing scares the adversary more than a woman who is on to him and knows how to crush him and access the power Jesus Christ offers her every day. I have learned to access that power and crush the enemy! It's not always easy, but every day gets better, and every day I learn just a little bit more."* (A Warrior Mother)

#3 - Hear Your Truth
Learn to differentiate between the Spirit's truth and Satan's lies.

Everyone is acquainted with some measure of loneliness, despair, grief, pain or sorrow. It is part of our life's purpose and journey. Often our challenges can eclipse the joy we are seeking. Lehi teaches us that we are meant to have joy: *"Adam fell that men might be; and men are, that they might have joy"* (2 Nephi 2:25). When we are going through difficult times, it is hard to believe God created us with the purpose of giving us joy, because we can feel like we will never be happy again.

Our enemy can cause us to get confused about God's eternal plan of happiness and our divine identity and purpose. Our enemy uses our vulnerability in our pain and confusion to tell us lies that we are alone, broken, doing everything wrong, unloved by God and weak. He wants us to believe God's plan is one "of misery and endless wo" (Helaman 5:12) as he points out our inability to overcome our challenges or help our children. Our enemy tricks us to believe our weaknesses or inabilities define us, and he equates enduring to the end with some form of heavenly torture meant to refine us.

We know success comes in knowing who we are, why we fight against darkness, who we fight for...and especially who fights by our side. We are children of a loving and powerful God. His promises of victory in our personal battles, healing of our wounds sustained in battle and ultimately winning the war against the enemy that assails us, are sure.

This is eternal truth. We are warriors who fight for the great cause of truth and

We are **PREPARING** our children for battle, **ARMING** them with the **KNOWLEDGE** they need as **WARRIORS** who are meant to fight in a war zone that is unpredictable and never fair.

freedom our Savior championed for us. We must never forget we chose, in an eternal realm, our side and who we would follow because we love our God, we love our families and we love our freedom. We chose to accept and fight for our Father's great plan and follow our Champion into battle because we are confident in His promises and ability to save us. We chose not only to accept God's great gift of agency but to fight for it. We are lovers of freedom and are agents unto ourselves. Lucifer seeks to

27

destroy our confidence in this decision. He is still trying to prove we don't deserve our agency and that the Father's plan and our Savior's promises are unsure. Christ is our captain and trainer in battle. He is our medic and healer. He is our Savior in war as He makes it possible for us to carry what is required and show up to the fight in a powerful and purposeful way every day because we know He goes before us and has our back. All we have to do is show up with intention, remembering we are eternal warriors for Jesus Christ in this war to win. We must stay awake to our enemy and his tactics lest we forget and fall. We must learn to discern what is truth and what is a lie.

Here are some examples:

Satan's lie: If I work hard enough and be perfect enough, I can save my whole family from bondage.

A Warrior's Truth: *There is only one Savior and it's not me!* I believe in God's power to heal and know how to support people in their battles in a powerful and meaningful way that encourages healing. Ultimately, it is the Savior who can save.

Satan's lie: What is wrong with you? You need to get it together! You are making life worse for everyone! You are broken and no one needs you because you just seem to make things harder for everyone. Perhaps this family would be better off without you.
A Warrior's Truth: I am strong in the Lord and in the power of His might. I am not broken or lost. I can add value to the lives of those I love in amazing ways as I rely upon Christ and how He magnifies me and heals me. I am not a quitter!

Satan's lie: You are such a loser. Everyone is better than you are and you have nothing of value to offer. Don't do anything to reveal what a mess you are.
A Warrior's Truth: I am a son/daughter of the living God. I am never alone and only God defines who I am. His is the only opinion that matters and I will believe in the courage and growth I can have with Him by my side.

Satan's lie: You are out of control. You're just embarrassing. Everyone is judging you. You should leave before they see just how weak you are. You need to play small so you don't mess up. Other people do amazing things, not you.

A Warrior's Truth: *"I can do all things through Christ which strengtheneth me"* (Philippians 4:13). When I feel anger or fear, I can do things to the enemy that cause him great pain - like work hard <u>on purpose</u> to make others' lives better, serve and love. I can be the me God tells me I am. God makes weaknesses strong and can use me just the way I am right now to bless my family as He performs His great work for the success of me and my family.

Satan's lie: You didn't sign up for this! Why are you putting up with them and their weaknesses, they just make your life harder! If they would just get it together you could change and be better. As long as you are with them you are going to be stuck and unhappy. What is wrong with them anyway? They don't love you or they wouldn't do that. You don't belong here, there is more happiness for you over there.

A Warrior's Truth: I only have one enemy and it is not my spouse/child/neighbor/boss/friend. Satan is the only enemy I have and he is very motivated to destroy my life, my love and my happiness. I can discern his lies and will always defend myself and those I love with the courage of a warrior of Jesus Christ. We choose Christ and His help, not you and your lame lies!

Satan's lie: Oh, my word, you need to get a clue! You can't get anything right. You don't know what to do or how to do it, so don't start. Don't ask for help because then they will know how weak and stupid you are. This is too big, too overwhelming for you. You'll never get it all done—may as well not try! I think there is one more bag of chocolate chips in the cupboard, just eat them. You need to just go watch TV, go shopping, quit, stop trying.

A Warrior's Truth: I was born for greatness. As a child of the living God, I have endless abilities and potential. I am not afraid to ask for advice, support, assistance or counsel because I know God is inspiring others to be angels in my life to help me find my way. God can answer prayers through other people. My purpose and vision are glorious. I am going to do great things that are perfect just for me and do it in the way I am meant to do them, not like anyone else.

Satan's lie: You are unlovable. No one understands you or wants you. You make others uncomfortable and don't fit in. You should leave before you reveal how worthless you are. Don't let anyone see you cry or your weakness. No one wants you or cares to help you. Can't you see the patterns and evidence in your life that prove people only pretend to love you so they can use you? You are all alone and always will be.

A Warrior's Truth: I know Heavenly Father loves me and has a beautiful plan for me. I am magnified through Christ's grace. I believe I am powerful with Him and will fight the enemy who is trying to stop me and convince me I am worthless. I am worth worlds! My Savior died just for me...to save me and protect me because I have such endless worth. I focus to see my great worth through Him. No matter how long it takes, I will walk with Christ as my best friend and allow Him to help me find the courage I desire for success. I LOVE HIM AND HE LOVES ME.

Notice how subtle and deceptive Satan can be with various thoughts in your head. Don't listen to those thoughts. Your loving Heavenly Father would NEVER talk to you that way. Combat those negative lies with your own TRUTH!

In *Mothers Who Know* we have a powerful message we declare often: STAY IN YOUR TRUTH! It reminds us to be discerning of the tormenting thoughts in our minds that belittle us and make us feel like all is lost and we are never going to be able to handle it because we are too weak and making a big mess as we try.

The truth is that we are supposed to be messy, look messy and make lots of messes. It's actually part of Heavenly Father's plan for our success. He knew we would automatically have weaknesses in our earthly, mortal experience because we are carnal/natural and prone to weakness. There is no way, never a way, for us to do it exactly right by ourselves. That's why He provided a Savior for us. All messes and mistakes are a call to us from our Father and His Son through the whisperings of the Holy Ghost, inviting us to remember them, come find them and rely on the glorious plan for our success they have for us. We can only carry our weakness in productive and powerful ways through their mercy, grace and power.

I invite you to allow the Spirit to testify to you that your truth is glorious and beautiful in His sight. Nothing you do, that is less than perfect in any way, changes that. Your worth is infinite! We often hear "you are enough." This is absolutely true with Christ's help...but there is something even truer. "Enough" doesn't begin to describe what you are. Our worth is unchanging and so is God's perfect love. As God's children, and with the Savior's help, we are infinitely more than enough! We should be saying, "Enough doesn't even describe me...*I am more than enough*!"

We teach a great tool that helps parents stay in their truth—Get ready, you're going to love this!

TRUTH Tool™

"Stay in your truth" is another way of saying: remember your divine identity and purpose. This tool is so helpful and allows you to stay in a place of remembering *who you are* and *whose you are*. Defend yourself from Satan's relentless efforts to get you to forget who you are, why you care and manipulate you into a place where you feel diminished.

Stay in Your

Terminate the lie
Restore the truth
Unite with God
THis is my weapon

Designate a notebook to catch the lies Satan tells you and turn them around. Start with one lie and keep numbering them. I promise as you do this your freedom will increase and your confidence will too. To stay connected with the truth about *who you are* and *whose you are*...first you must clean out all the lies that are in the way. With a little practice, this will become easier and soon you will notice how much more joy and peace you have in your life. You will be able to hear the real truth about yourself from our Heavenly Father and Jesus Christ. The love you feel in your life from them will increase and you will find PEACE!! It's worth every effort!

There are four steps that follow the acronym TRUTH - it's easy and so smart to do...

> **T - Terminate the lie:** Write down exactly what lie is in your head. A lie is anything you hear that you would never say out loud to anyone else because it would be so rude or inappropriate.
> **R - Restore the truth:** What would it sound like if God were speaking to you? (Turn the lie around to the exact opposite. Whether you believe it or not, write the truth about you. If you are having a hard time identifying the lie, start noticing any negative emotions you are having...the lies are under those emotions.)
> **U - Unite with God:** Say something that involves redeeming light...use the names of our Heavenly Father and Jesus Christ and who they are and why the truth you have with them and because of them, makes you amazing! You are a daughter/son of the living God!

TH - This is my weapon! Stick it to him (Satan)! Point out your powerful, beautiful, awesome body...the weapon he doesn't have and tell him how it ROCKS and that you love having one. Point out things about it you love and remember that even in its weakest state he would take it in a second. Get up and use your body to do righteous things to bless the lives of others. While you do so, let the enemy know that whenever you catch him messing with you, you're going to make him sorry he showed up.

Example #1:

T - Terminate the lie: *"You're terrible at speaking in front of people. You should shut your mouth and sit down. These people can see right through you. You are weak and scared and stupid."*
R - Restore the truth: *"I'm a fantastic speaker and I'm good at opening my mouth to reveal truth and diminish your lame lies."*
U - Unite with God: *"The truth is; 'I can do all things through Christ which strengtheneth me' (Philippians 4:13). 'He is [my] way, [my] truth, and [my] life!'" (John 14:6).*
TH - This is my weapon! *"Speaking of 'speaking'...there are so many cool things about my amazing mouth...with it I can speak kind words that cause you pain. I can eat delicious food like chocolate, grapes and warm bread. I can kiss my husband and make him feel handsome and happy. The most fun is when I use my mouth to smile! Wow...it's super sad you don't get a mouth...you are missing out!"* Now, go speak kind words to others and express your love for them and tell them how awesome they are.

Example #2:

T - Terminate the lie: *"You're worthless."*
R - Restore the truth: *"I am of infinite worth!"*
U - Unite with God: *"I have a loving Heavenly Father who gave me the plan of happiness and provided a Savior for me...even Jesus Christ, my elder brother, who died for me because I am of such great worth to Him."*

TH - This is my weapon! *"Speaking of my worth...I just wanted to point out that it's worth it to have a body. It is so worth it! A body is the best!" Then go prove it by doing something worth your time that makes you feel happy and full of energy...dance, sing, skip, jump on the trampoline and invite someone you love to join you— anything that makes you smile and be happy.*

Example #3:

T - Terminate the lie: *"You're so fat."*

R - Restore the truth: *~~"Excuse me?? I am not fat; I am fabulous in every way!"~~*

U - Unite with God: *"This is MY body! You have NO power here! Heavenly Father has given me power to crush you! My amazing body was created by God the Father and His Son Jesus Christ...it is beautiful and serves me very well. He goes before my radiant, confident face. He is on my beautiful right and left hand. His Spirit is in my faithful, courageous heart and His angels are round about me to bear me up!"* (D&C 84:88).

TH - This is my weapon! *"I shouted for joy when Father announced I could have this awesome body and so did you!! Too bad you didn't make very wise choices after that...because now you will never know what it feels like. It's just lame that you bring up that I am fat...you wish you were fat!!! Let out a shout for joy for your body, go to a mirror, smile and wink at yourself as you say: "Wow, I'm super cute and I have perfect (say the part of your body that you hear the most attacks/lies about). Thank you, Heavenly Father, for my terrific body."*

Practice! Fill your notebook with lies and use it as a prison where each time you close it, one more bully lie is taken out. The more you catch lies, point out your truth, add redeeming light and confidently state how cool your weapon is...the more your personal power and freedom will increase. Soon Satan's lies will be so obvious to you, that you will get super good at dismissing them immediately. You will even notice there are far fewer lies and negative thoughts in your head.

Your efforts with this tool will really pay off and your confidence in all areas of your life will increase, including your confidence before God. **Don't let Satan chip away at your confidence!** Stand in your truth by standing up to him! Don't let some old man create distance between you and God! Fight for your testimony, fight for your freedom, fight to feel all the peace, love and power that comes from being close to the Savior. Believe in all the promises He and our Father in Heaven have given you.

> I am a **sacred weapon** of
> **hope, faith,** and
> **endless works**
> designed to **inspire** and love.
> I can change the very tide of
> **battle.**

We are taught that we are not alone in our battle: *"Fear not: for they that be with us are more than they that be with them"* (2 Kings 6:16). We are meant to have joy and be confident in our stewardships as we have feelings of high self-worth, despite the challenges we face – NOT fear, doubt and a great lack of confidence. In 2 Timothy 1:7 we are taught about the kind of individuals God created us to be: "For God hath not given us the spirit of fear; but of power, and of love, and of a sound mind."

When we align ourselves with our Savior Jesus Christ, who is our greatest ally, we are empowered by how He magnifies our efforts in our battles. We have a proper perspective about how He sees us in our weakness. His perfect, loving role is to *always* be with us as we *remember* who He is and call upon Him for help.

YOU ARE LOVED AND CHERISHED!!!! Don't let anyone tell you any different!

(You can download a copy of the TRUTH Tool: www.bit.ly/truthtool)

"The reason my son came home in tears of relief, anger and a new determination from his second week attending his Sons of Helaman group is because he heard a truth that opposed the huge lie Satan had been working on for 6+ years to thwart my son's progress and belief in himself. He believed he was his own worst enemy - Satan had convinced him he was the enemy.

He believed he was weak and pathetic because he was dirty/deviant/unworthy in God's eyes. So whenever he tried to be a good guy he heard, 'You are a liar, a hypocrite, a poser...you know who you really are and you will never overcome this, because how can you win when you are your own worst enemy?' The lies would reinforce his cycle of lost battles and lost self-esteem, etc. But when he expressed to me in a tearful state I had never seen him in before or since, with fierce determination in his voice to kick the enemy in the tail and fight back, it was a game changer. He said, for the first time, 'Mom! I am not the enemy. I have an enemy, and it's NOT me!'"

#4 - Use a Team in the Fight
Just as your youth will need training and team support, so will you. Align yourself with a team!

In the Sons of Helaman program, clinician Maurice Harker teaches young men they need to align themselves with a team to get the support they need in their intense efforts to fight. If they think they can do it on their own, they are buying into the adversary's lie that they can do it all by themselves and don't need anyone to help. That's like a soldier in Vietnam thinking it's smart to run into the jungle to face an army of enemies by himself.

Sometimes the Savior is asking those who fight so hard to learn about what He has waiting for them on a team. When you are a parent supporting a loved one, don't try to do it alone! Get help and support. Get an army for yourself too.

There are lots of great places to get support and training, but I can't think of another organization that gives the vital and stellar support Life Changing Services does for parents. My opinion comes from being personally supported and trained by this organization and how this has blessed me and my family. I have also witnessed the transformation of hundreds of individuals who have been helped by the programs of Life Changing Services.

I invite you to experience this unique, cutting edge training which courageously goes right to the heart of the issues. This training will empower you to take back the control you have lost and replace it with confidence, self-mastery and purposeful living at a level you never dreamed possible. You will finally be connecting the dots of knowledge you have always had in a way that ignites your divinity. Success will come on many levels as you purposefully recognize what is important to you.

With **INTENSE FEROCITY** we will determine to stand together to face our adversary. As we **UNITE,** it is much easier to remember who we are, what we are fighting for and why it's so important to **NEVER GIVE UP!**

When my family found Life Changing Services and enrolled our son in the Sons of Helaman program, finding recovery for our son was all we were hoping for. I had no idea the training he was receiving would change my life as well. As I learned to apply the same principles my son was learning to my own unwanted patterns of behavior, amazing things happened to me. I noticed as I gained appreciation for this useful and highly applicable information, my ability to love myself, love my life and love the messes in it improved. I learned new skills I could use to approach my personal battles in powerful ways.

These skills and tools enhance all the glorious truth I have in the gospel of Jesus Christ. In a sense, the principles of learning to fight and win battles connected dots I hadn't realized were disconnected. I could be a more purposeful disciple who understood how to better remember Christ and how to follow Him.

My perspective changed. I was healing!

I went from feeling like a big mess and being the cause of that mess, to realizing there was a big bully messing with me so he could get to my family more easily. I realized why a parent would be a formidable target and that I could fight back, and even cause Satan pain with my new skills.

Any good military strategist will try to take the captains out first to win the war. I am a captain/leader for my family. I am to train, teach, protect, defend and know how to find and call proper medical attention when my little band is wounded. [Please look into our *Eternal Warriors Training*, it is patterned after the Sons of Helaman program for those who want to learn how to use the same principles for personal self-mastery. For information, go to www.eternalwarriorstraining.org]

It is powerful to be part of a faithful team that stands in the storm facing the enemy with faith in the Savior. The fastest way to increase our power is to rid ourselves of isolation and come to a safe place where there is light, faith, love and truth.

"I joined a training class online for parents of boys who were new to the [Sons of Helaman] program even though my son wasn't yet enrolled. This is where, for the first time, I heard other parents speak about their child's journey. It was like they were relating our story almost exactly! Bright, confident, popular, athletic, gifted, leader and other descriptive words were used to describe the children in the program. I cried listening to them relate the pain their children were experiencing and the frustration they felt as parents. We all felt guilt for having been naïve. For the first time I shared our story with someone outside of our tight circle and it felt amazing! I was so impressed with the powerful spirit the counselor had when she educated us. We were taught to remove the shame and blame from our innocent children and to put it squarely on the shoulders of the adversary where it belongs." (Fisher, *http://bit.ly/redeeminglight*)

I often picture mothers standing/leaning beautifully into this storm - looking formidable, as the lioness at the gate, as if saying, "You messed with the wrong mom! We know who we are! We have no doubt who our sons and daughters are! We see who you are and it's nothing compared to the miraculous delivering power of our Champion and Savior!"

"In the lowest of times, I understand now how Satan was really working hardest on me. I can honestly say that he had attacked me so fiercely that I could see absolutely NOTHING but the bad in my son. I could hardly even speak to him or look at him, without feeling that he will never get out of his addiction to Mr. M [masturbation].

He would never be able to serve a mission. He would fail at everything and all I could see in him was a dirty minded young man with unclean thoughts and he was being a bad young man in everything he did. I could only think the worst! And assume the worst.

Wow! That is hard and what horrible things to write about a child. Don't wanna go there again! The lowest part for me was when I realized how tired and exhausted I was. How pessimistic I was and I really didn't like myself. Nor did I think anyone liked me either.

Satan sure knows how to attack our weaknesses.

So, the change started to take place after I took an Eternal Warriors class and also learned tools in Mothers Who Know. I learned the tools to fight Satan!

I learned - there are 3 businesses:

1. God's business

2. Your business (my son's)

3. ~~My Business.~~ Which is the Only One I have control over.

That was liberating for me!

I let go of trying to "fix him" and focused on my own weaknesses, realizing it's taken me 30+ years to get over my own issues. I was fighting back and letting Satan know I was going to take control of my thoughts and look for and see the GOOD in others and let my son know how proud I am of him. As I was able to do this, I began assuming the best and treating him with the pure love of Christ.

At Christmas time we asked our family this question. What gift has the Savior given you this year? Our son's answer was "The Gift of Example. Example of friends and family living the Gospel." It was a gift to us to hear him say that.

My gift was the Gift of Peace. I had turned it over to God's Business and worked on myself instead of my son. And I received peace!

I see him now, like I would want God to see me. I stopped comparing him too to others. We try to be consistent with reading the Book of Mormon, having family prayer and attending the temple weekly!

I know we will always need to stay alert and keep our guard up. Pray always! Prayers have a LOT of power. Don't forget to pray for eyes to see with Heavenly Father's perspective, not only for our sons...but for yourself.

Sincerely,

A Mother in the fight!"

#5 - Remember Who and Whose You Are
You are powerful!

I don't think we are parents in this day by chance, nor do I think our children are here at this time and in our care at random. I believe we are here during this intense, modern day spiritual war because we are the spirits reserved for this particular time. We are the parents of these amazing children, at this exact time, for a very specific reason known to our Father in Heaven. Because of the intensity of our spirits and the ferocious ability we have to stand with and for the Savior against a beguiling bully, we are here in this time and place.

When I realized how I had unknowingly given the adversary more power than I wanted to and why I was a target, it was liberating to then *wake up the warrior* inside of me, the warrior I had always been and could be now. I defeated Satan with the words of my testimony in the pre-earth life, and now, with training and the Spirit, I could still stand in this second estate armed with a weapon Satan does not have, my body.

As a daughter of God and an *intentional* parent who knows the power I have in my stewardship, I am on the front lines for Father. I am a steward and vessel for Him as He is

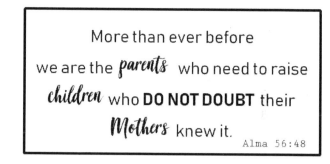

More than ever before we are the *parents* who need to raise *children* who **DO NOT DOUBT** their *Mothers* knew it.
Alma 56:48

extending His work and glory to bring to pass the eternal success of me and my family (Moses 1:39). He will never leave us alone in this great and important work with our families. I trust Him and know His arm is not weak. He is performing miracles, signs and wonders among those who have faith in Him. I can order Satan to "go play in traffic" and remind him who I am and why he will not have my family! I can declare our power in Christ as we join Him in defense of His great cause of freedom.

When Satan is attacking our children and they are losing battles, having a seemingly impossible time at winning, it's tempting to lose faith and hope. Now, because of the principles and skills I have learned, I'm better equipped to stand in a place of strength and faith. I'm armed with an understanding of the divine power of our Savior within my child and a stronger belief in God's plan and our Savior's promises to heal and rescue my child.

Create a Personal Declaration

I'd like to share a technique we use to keep our minds in a place of strength and faith as we join the Savior in His great cause of freedom. This involves creating your own personal declaration which you say aloud as you stand in front of the mirror each morning (alone is usually less intimidating, but the choice is yours).

A parent's Declaration might sound like this:

> "Enemy beware! You are messing with the wrong mom/dad. I am [your name here], a daughter/son of the living God. I am a fearless warrior disciple for Jesus Christ. I stand strong with Him in defense of this family to protect our freedom. We are the [your last name here] - your worst celestial nightmare. Because of Heavenly Father's great Plan of Happiness and eternal covenants that connect us to our Savior and Champion Jesus Christ, we have nothing to fear, but you have everything to fear as we build upon our Rock and Redeemer. We are leaning into your storms and will not fall because you are no match for the Savior. He is Christ, the Son of God, and we are His disciples... standing with Him to crush you."

A Declaration might sound something like this for a daughter:

> "Enemy beware! An amazing daughter of the living God stands here. She is aligned with her truth and knows her power and how to get more. Any who seek to destroy her will have to deal with her Protector and Champion, Jesus Christ. She is armed for battle - arrayed in her divine beauty and spiritual armor - she does not fear. Her battle cry is: 'Bring it...at all times and in all things and in all places! I love God and He loves me, and you are going down!' She confidently whispers, 'Be afraid...be very afraid! You are messing with the wrong warrior disciple of Christ.' She will hurt

you - she will destroy you - she will crush you!! Turn back, or die trying to mess with this daughter of God!"

A Declaration for your son could be:

"Enemy beware! Here stands a noble son of God who is strong in the Lord and the power of His might. His armor is worn and tested but shining with the preparation and skill of the formidable warrior you fear. He is an annoyer and disturber to your cause, endowed with the power to act in Christ's name. His is the voice you fear as he inspires others to arms in Christ's great cause of liberty and eternal life for all. He is honored and called up to serve Christ, the Champion over all darkness. His battle cry is 'Victory through Christ, Jesus – freedom for all!!' Never will he stop defending others from your sick lies and tactics. He will crush you and stand forever to testify against the darkness you are...Be afraid – you are messing with a leader and asset in God's noblest army. Fear this son of God - he can see you and, like a sniper, will take you out at the slightest movement you make in his direction."

I hope you can see how this is similar to the way David spoke to Goliath or Captain Moroni spoke to Zarahemna at the waters of Sidon. I hope you can also see how such declarations will trigger your Warrior Chemistry, a tool the young men learn in Sons of Helaman groups to win their mood battles. (Warrior Chemistry explained: As moods/feelings increase, we don't notice that on the even more subtle level, our chemical levels are changing in the brain. The more negative feelings grow, the more the brain energy moves from the frontal lobe [Values] and toward the middle brain [Survival]. If you are going to win a psychological battle with Satan, you will need clear chemicals and you will need to be in your frontal lobe! You will need to shift your brain chemistry first. We do that by shifting into a mood or set of feelings that are more useful.)

43

"*Speaking of time, I didn't know in the beginning how long the road ahead of us would be or the painful relapses we were to experience when we made the determination to get him [our son] help. I couldn't see from my perspective then, the pain and anguish of the refiner's fire we needed to go through to ultimately strengthen him and us, to keep fighting and to never give up. We never gave up even when in a fit of rage one night he destroyed the stair railing in our home during a confrontation with his father. It is hard to forget how tortured he looked during these times. We never gave up even when he worked tirelessly for years with ecclesiastical leaders to overcome his addiction (we are so thankful our ward Bishop and leaders loved him unconditionally; the way the Savior would. In the end, this was the best thing they could have done for him). Even though the journey was perilous and we couldn't see the end, we just never gave up. It was our faith in God...that was the key to our survival. We had to believe, God willing, our son could be whole. He wasn't broken or a lost cause, nor would he be forsaken.*" (Fisher, http://bit.ly/redeeminglight)

#6 - Believe in Your Son or Daughter
Your children are sons and daughters of God. They are entitled to receive divine help.

"HERE, LET ME HELP YOU CLEAN THAT UP." When our kids were little and would go outside to play and then come in covered in dirt, mud, etc., we still loved them. The dirt didn't matter to us. We would just help them to clean up so a bigger mess didn't occur. When our children grow up and are living their lives out in the world, they will also get dirt on them, but the same principle applies...LOVE THEM! We know how to assist them to clean things up before a bigger mess happens, and we will still always love them and be glad they allowed us to help them clean it up.

Children are smart and equipped from the pre-existence to face the intensity of the opposition in this day. Often, we forget that while just a generation before them, our definition of the training they need and what they are ready to discuss to keep them safe, may be way too conservative. When they go out into the world they cannot avoid all the sexual messages and images. They must be trained and prepared to be exposed to such things. Warn them of dangers – train them what to do when they are in danger. If we saw a snake in the grass or bushes, would we not warn them?

Then as they move ahead, cheer for and compliment them. Our children, especially those in recovery, need to be told they are smart, in charge of their heart and brain, and they are strong enough to take what the world throws at them. They need to know that despite all this, they can stand tall with hope, power and light because they know who the Savior is and how to use His power.

Satan is **screaming...**

Why are WE whispering?

Satan and his minions are screaming...why then are we whispering? When we talk about the opposition in our day, we need to also counteract it with who God is and what his great plan provides for us. *"And we talk of Christ, we rejoice in Christ, we preach of Christ, we prophesy of Christ, and we write according to our prophecies, that our children may know to what source they may look for a remission of their sins"* (2 Nephi 25:26).

We must talk much more about Christ and His victory over the world than we do about how much we fear the world and its darkness. We need

45

to exemplify our hope in Christ and boldly speak, especially about light. What if we were to speak just as much or more about what is going *right* in our children's lives, our family or the world? We can use this kind of energy to point out that we can look forward to a brighter day.

There will be people in our families who sustain wounds, some very deep, despite our efforts to warn and teach them. We always hope they will avoid danger. But the enemy is good at what he does and he is aware of the danger our loved one is to his plan of misery. When wounds show up at your house, you must focus on speaking boldly. Be positive. Look for the good. Remember wounds take time to heal. We must allow Christ to do His job. Tell your child they are going to figure this out and that no matter how many times they say they can't do it and don't deserve it, you testify with your love and cheerfulness that the Savior and Champion of all our battles says differently. He gave *all* to prove your child's worth and you are never going to believe they can't do it. Because you are their mother, you know how amazing they are—they must be...or Satan wouldn't be working so hard to defeat them. The stripling warriors fought with courage and faith, but they also sustained wounds along the way. Wounds heal.

As a mother, I found that most times I felt inadequate in what to say to my son and rarely felt like I said things right. But I do know that the Spirit really helped me because of my effort to trust the above process when my son really needed it. Bottom line, never stop cheering and believing in your son or daughter. They will make it, even if it's not always in our preferred timeline.

"Nineteen weeks is how long it took my son to graduate from his program. Nineteen weeks where he studied, practiced, tried and failed and tried again. Those nineteen weeks, plus six years, is how long he had to live by faith that he could be healed; before he finally was. During that time he developed patience, long-suffering and a compassion for others I doubt would have developed under "normal" circumstances. I would have done anything to save him

from the pain he had to endure, but he is stronger because of it. He is closer to his Savior Jesus Christ and he knows He has been with him, even in the darkest hours. It was ultimately He, who healed my son.

While he was in the program I had to let go of control and let the One who really knows my son take over. I became my son's biggest fan and cheerleader! We rallied around him as a family and cheered him on, every step of the way. I no longer inquired about every little thing he did and every decision he made. I just reminded him he had a Savior and encouraged him to turn to Him. I also had to learn to fight in a different way. I began to strengthen myself against the enemy and looked diligently in the scriptures for answers to help me stay faithful and close to the Savior. My prayers became more focused on increasing my faith which was strengthened and then something unexpected happened. I found peace! How I had longed to have peace! I believed I would never have it again because I thought I had to keep punishing myself for what had happened to my son. Instead, I had to forgive myself. I had to hand it all over to the Lord. He truly lifts our burdens even if he doesn't remove them entirely. We had to rely on his redeeming light to dispel the dark.

Although I had my son back, I had to let go of the idea of a perfect son and being a perfect mother. No one is perfect! We all make mistakes and we are each given different trials, but we also have what we need to overcome them with us already. It's just a decision to fight or to give up each day. If I could give a word of advice to parents who find themselves in a situation like mine, it would be to look in the mirror first, before criticizing a son or daughter over their mistakes. Just be proud of them for choosing to fight and even for just showing up for battle. I wish I had done this more and had not continued to bring up his past mistakes. I had my own low-level addictions to conquer, and I still do! I have learned from my son. The teacher has indeed become the student. My son and the other youth in recovery inspire me! They are amazing! Their strength pitted against their enemy; a 7,000 year old military, social, physiological and psychological genius opponent, to me is incredible!!" (Fisher, http://bit.ly/redeeminglight)

#7 - Listen with the Spirit
What works for one person may not be what works for you. Let the Spirit guide you to what works best for you, your family and your unique situation.

As we begin (or continue) this journey of recovery with our loved one, it can be easy to get frustrated and wonder why things are not working for us and our situation. It can be overwhelming at times. There will be days you just want to curl up and not get out of bed because of the things you have to face that day. You may even read this, try a few things and think—this is NOT working for me! What am I doing wrong? I did it exactly like it says in there!

Remember you have stewardship over your family, and you have the privilege of receiving inspiration for your family and your situation. The Lord will help you. As you read these things and receive training, listen with the Spirit to those things that are for you. Not everything will be for you, and not everything will work exactly the same in your family. But take the advice and tips from others who have been in your shoes, try things out, see what feels right and works for you and let the Lord guide you to answers specific to your family.

There are currently thousands of warrior mothers out there fighting a battle similar to yours, but each has a unique way of battling and a unique way of hearing what will work for them. Sometimes we need to change and adapt over time. Sometimes the things that work today won't work a week from now. But know that you have been called to be your child's mother, and the Lord will not leave you alone. Your child is also His child. *"This is MY work and MY glory"* (Moses 1:39). Our loving Father in Heaven will teach us along the way. He will help us hear and understand exactly what we need to hear to help our children. He can be our teacher as we walk this incredible journey of healing, recovery, humility, teaching and ultimately, peace—however that looks for each of us. We can all learn to stand strong in the storms of life and walk through them, *even feeling happiness along the way*, with the help of the Spirit. With His help, we can know the best way to handle things at our house, with our formula, in our way, however that looks.

Please read through some helpful suggestions from other warrior mothers who have walked this same road and fought many of the same battles you are facing. Listen with the Spirit to what will work for you and for the things that you need to hear right now. Know you don't have to fight alone. You not only have the Savior on your side...you have an entire force of righteous mothers fighting alongside you, even if you can't see them.

The following are helpful suggestions from our "Mothers Who Know":

- **Get dressed in the armor of God like you mean it. Use a MOM PoWeR* calendar for yourself. Be transparent about your challenges and let your child know you are working on things too.** Before you show up as a parent, you need to be dressed for battle. Armor up! Are you doing your MOM PoWeR* goals at meaningful and consistent levels to enable you to win your personal battles? One of the greatest things you can do is set up your own goals and calendar and put them next to your warrior youth's calendar. Fight the war side by side instead of face to face. Let your child see that you make mistakes and have to work at the calendar too. This process is very validating and can be fun. There are very few things more humbling or more powerful than doing your own MOM PoWeR calendar and then reviewing it with your young warrior. (*See calendar in appendix.)

- **Remember, acquiring training for your child and yourself is healthy and wise.** You will be tempted to police all things, make sure your child is following the program and have a hyper-focus on all things recovery. If you approach your child's recovery in this way, you will make yourself sick and neglect other important stewardships. Don't fall for that. Instead, focus on your strengths, and what you can contribute. I had to realize I was not a brain surgeon, nor could I be a clinician. I could not save my son, that would be Christ. My son needed someone who knew how to work with the scientific side of self-mastery (a clinician). He needed pressure and motivation, and that comes from the Personal Warrior Trainer. I needed to learn my role as a parent was primarily as a cheerleader and fellow warrior.

- **Know how to clean house (in your mind) and dump your trash.** When the enemy was not attacking, the Nephites made preparations for war. They guarded things, built great fortresses, fortified walls, forged their armor, stored provisions, made weapons to defend, set watchmen on towers and practiced their drills. Learn how to best plan, build, practice, fortify, prepare, defend and put protections in place for the storms or attacks which will come your way.

- **Remember, you can be the captain like unto Moroni for your loved ones.** You can be a walking "title of liberty" by often repeating why you are fighting your battles. You can lead as Moroni did by working on your own self-mastery. Show how you, with your sound understanding, can also bind Satan and train others to do the same.

- **Acknowledge the formula that makes up your family has unique ingredients.** Everything you learn from your training and support here has to fit into the mix that makes up your amazing family. Don't be in such a panic to hurry up and heal that you can't consider all things in the spirit and how they will affect your formula and your ingredients. You can go overboard trying to heal your child by taking them off sugar or using healing oils or planting your whole yard in a garden just because you hear it was the answer for someone else. You and God are in charge of your healing. Only He completely understands how all the ingredients work and fit into your family formula. Nothing a clinician, bishop, book, fellow parent or warrior recommends can truly be the answer for you until it is something you and God decide will work for you. Ask God in faith and the best formula for your family will be revealed to you through the spirit of revelation. Your formula will be awesome and unique to your family and what God knows you need!

- **Don't compare your journey with that of others or make judgment calls on whether you are failing or not.** Just because someone else is further along in their healing and/or recovery than you are, put your trust in God's timing. He is doing His work with you and your family and knows just how to bring about your success. It is His great glory (Moses 1:39). He's got this and you!

- **Acknowledge addiction is real.** I realized I could not save my son alone. We were here for a reason. My child needed someone who was trained and knew how to work with the scientific side of self-mastery and addiction so he could get the support he needed to win and recover.

- **Talk to your son or daughter's clinician.** Keep the clinician informed of your concerns. If you feel your warrior is lying, let the clinician know. If there are other patterns of misbehavior (i.e. disrespect in the home, struggles in school), keep the clinician informed. They do their best work when they have more information. Occasionally, as needed, set up a full therapy session with the clinician for your own training and to learn what he is doing specifically with your young warrior.

- **Set up an appointment to visit with your child's bishop** (This applies if your child is still a youth.) Don't wait for the bishop to contact you. Don't assume your bishop is well trained in how to work with addictions. Respectfully request he shares with you what his plan is for your youth. Respectfully request being informed of what his expectations are for your youth. Respectfully offer more information about working with addictions if he feels insufficiently informed. Respectfully request a certain frequency of visits you would like him to have with your youth. Inform the bishop of how you want sensitive topics to be discussed with your youth, especially daughters, i.e. masturbation. (Note: Feel free to refer him to us to request free resources for ecclesiastical leaders. www.lifechangingservices.org/sonsofhelaman/resources/bishops-resources/)

- **Recognize your child is noble and strong. You are a parent to this cool child.** The fact you are here needing support does not define you or your child. Only God defines us, not all the evidence of our success or failure. He is very aware of the desires of your heart and holds you and your child in the greatest esteem and place of love!

- **Know you are doing so many things right.** Don't let this challenge you face be the only thing you notice. With the Savior, broken people can do amazing things in a very broken way. The same goes for your child. Make a conscious effort to talk about more than what is going wrong or what you are afraid of. Fight for your child by increasing the positive things they notice – Satan is constantly pointing out what they are doing wrong, don't you do it too.

- **Remember you only have one enemy.** Satan is the father of all lies, including the lies he tells us about those we love and fight for. Your enemy is not your child who is causing the pain you feel, or your spouse who doesn't seem to get how important it is to support your child in a better, more involved or nurturing way, or the person whose fault it is your child started down a road to addiction. We only have one enemy, and it is never people we care for and defend.

- **Remind yourself not every voice in your head is a trusted voice.** Consider what has gone on over the years inside your head and what has affected your abilities, courage, choices and outcomes. Satan wants you to think you are small. He wants you to only play small and never go big. When you know how to identify his lies, the real you begins to show up. You can start to play big as you recognize the pain he has been trying to inflict upon you by lying to you. As you stand in your truth, he becomes very small.

- **Stay in your own battle.** There are only three kinds of business...my business, your business and God's business. I will always be miserable when I try to get in someone else's battle/business and think I need to swing their sword and hold their shield. We are all meant to wield our own weapons for a wise and eternal purpose. Only Satan would convince us we are to force, control, boss or manipulate others so they are successful. That is Satan's plan. Aren't we glad we chose liberty and eternal life, not captivity and death? Staying in our own battle and letting others learn to fight theirs will always promote liberty as we rely upon our strength in the Lord and the power of His might.

- **Cheer your guts out.** Point out everything you notice about your child that would make them a formidable target to the enemy. Tell your child how scary they are to the dark side and what an asset they are to God's army. Specifics are always more powerful.

- **Ask your child to teach you what they are learning.** Ask to sincerely learn, not to interrogate or challenge. This will validate and show respect for your child as well as help solidify what they are learning in group and in their personal efforts. Don't become the teacher in your discussions, be the student. If your child does not seem to know the answers, tell them you look forward to learning more in the future. Then tell them, "until next time."

- **Stimulate conversations with the Holy Ghost for your child.** Often, we have a voice which can shut down warrior type thinking because we are the parent and our child is going through an individuation process in their development. Why not make it harder for Satan to mess with your child by stimulating conversations that allow your youth to have a conversation with the best teacher - our Heavenly Father, through his spokesman, the Holy Ghost? The Holy Ghost brings important things to mind, helps us remember our divine nature, testifies of truth, tells us all things we must do and helps us to feel God's love and be sanctified in our trials. **Suggestions:** *Ask meaningful questions.* "Are you pleased with your progress?" and then walk away letting the accountability be to God and the Holy Ghost, not you. *Use positive assumptions.* "I was just about to ask you if you were going to do your PoWeR goals, but then I remembered you are the kind of person who knows what power is and where to find more." *Express random meaningful compliments.* "Man, I like the person you are becoming. Your courage is such an asset to God's army." *Testify of truth.* "I'm so glad we have a Savior who can really save us, aren't you?" *Drop love notes.* Take your voice and face out of it and just allow them to soak in the joy of hearing your unconditional love and then ponder what you say in the spirit. *Send a text.* "Thank you for always caring for your sister and looking after her. I feel so blessed to have a child who makes me feel another level of safety because I know how much you love and protect her. Wow, you are going to make a spouse very safe and happy one day. Keep up the great work my child." *Wake up the warrior.* Many lose battles in their bedrooms. One of our amazing mothers would say goodnight in a meaningful way: "Have a good night, my Warrior." Many lose battles in the bathroom, so say: "Have a great Warrior Shower." Don't tease or demean in sarcasm. Be genuine and unconditional and their warrior brain will shift.

In

WAR

you can't avoid

BATTLE

- **Don't panic when your child loses battles.** Hold on and have faith in the process. Remember, in order for them to become a consistent winner they have to become good at bouncing back after a lost battle. To win long term, a warrior needs to know how to spring back, analyze what went wrong, and get back in the fight with increased determination and insight. In this process, your child will gain more reliance upon the Lord and increased confidence in their ability to win long term.

- **Always testify you know who your daughter or son is.** Only great things define them. How they respond to this challenge is refining them and making them better.

- **Make a purposeful and detailed study of the war chapters of the** *Book of Mormon* **(Alma 43-63).** You will learn so much about how to improve your ability to fight in this modern day spiritual war we face. The war chapters truly were written to instruct us in our modern-day battles and to help us defeat the enemy of our souls.

- **Recall we live in the last days when prophets have foretold this great spiritual war we face.** In great wars, there are lots of wounds, especially among the most valiant of warriors. This war is not for wimps! ALL will need to turn to Christ, whom we followed into this battle. Jesus Christ is our captain, medic, trainer, champion and has claimed our victory. Satan is no match for the Savior and we are here because we believe in Christ and His promise to defend, protect and save us. We chose to follow Him and fight with Him for His great cause of freedom and victory over death so we can have all our Father has. When Satan whispers to you it is too hard, you did not sign up for this or you have too much evidence at your house/in your life you are losing the war, etc. stand and declare as Nephi did in 2 Nephi 4:30-35. We are not wimps, we are warriors!!! We need only wake up the warrior we have always been, claim our birthright and embrace our calling to fight this most important of wars. Parents are SO IMPORTANT in this great cause! We must remember who we are and whose side we are on. When we "Warrior Up" and speak of ourselves and our loved ones as the warriors we truly are for these latter-days, miraculous things happen! I have seen it in my own life and in many others. You are in God's great powerful army...claim your spot. You have been offered the firmest of foundations in Christ, the Son of God...if we stand with Him, we cannot fall.

- **Be so very patient and forgiving of yourself and always consider each moment, hour, day is all you have right now.** Don't let the adversary trick you into looking way behind you in regret, shame and blame or way in front of you in fear, doubt, overwhelming confusion and frustration. Stay right where you are and remember the Spirit only works and inspires in the "now." Trust your divine ability and calling. With God you are *plenty* - and *more than enough* to do anything this situation asks of you; just do it with HIM.

- **Be transparent.** There is great power waged against the dark side when we are willing to be honest and transparent with our children about the fact that we, too, have lost battles. We don't have to reveal every skeleton in our closet, but it is important to let them know you believe in the power of healing and know people can learn and grow because you have. Especially be transparent and honestly apologize when your children see you lose battles. Don't listen when Satan is telling you it's better to "save face" and it's ok for your child to see you hiding in shame and darkness. Instead, show your courage and humility to your child as you bring dark things into the light where they can be healed. Be a fellow warrior and fight shoulder to shoulder, facing the same enemy, not face to face against each other.

- **Absolutely enlist in the Eternal Warriors Training.** As you apply the effective principles your child is learning to your own unwanted patterns of misbehavior, you will have increased respect and empathy for what your child faces and the hard work it takes to win their battles. You will wake up fully to the war you are in and how personal it is. You will understand the scientific and spiritual side of self-mastery that will empower you. Your level of spiritual discernment and ability to receive personal revelation will increase. You will learn specific tactics the adversary is using to distract and deceive you and your family and how to fight back. You will wake up the warrior you have always been and feel rocking awesome!

- **Recognize God's ways are not our ways.** God has a different calendar and clock than we do. We can get very impatient and lose lots of hope and faith when we think they are the same. Trust Him, lean not on your understanding, acknowledge Him and let him direct your life. (Proverbs 3:5-6)

- **Don't forget the adversary is a tormenter and you are the terminator!** Whenever you are feeling negative emotions getting stronger, you are under attack. Fear, doubt, despair, negative self judgment, feeling overwhelmed, etc. are all spun by the adversary to get you in a mood battle that will lead to a lost battle. *A lost battle is anything you do or say that is not within your value system.* Fight back with your drills and warrior chemistry (Eternal Warriors Training).

> I am a **sacred weapon** of
> **hope, faith,** and
> **endless works**
> designed to **inspire** and love.
> I can change the very tide of
> **battle**.

- **Recognize when others are under attack.** There is no need to get in your child's battles or become afraid. You have power to enhance their ability in battle and diminish Satan's power IF you are not pulled into it. You can do awesome things to shift the mood of a room (remember you are the atmosphere angel) in a way that is attention-getting and you don't have to say anything about the fact they are under attack. Remember they are figuring out how to fight with and for the Savior and you are doing the same by being on the amazing support team. You are on the front lines of support in God's work with your loved one. Your efforts, reactions and word choice can enhance this work. Do all the cool things you do for your warrior in the Lord's name to promote His work with your son or daughter. Hand your warrior water bottles from God, make favorite treats, do silent, random acts of service, all in an effort to let the enemy know you discern him (Satan) messing with your loved one and you will do what is in your power to decrease his power.

- **Get involved in *Mothers Who Know* or *Fathers Who Fight* and listen to the parent trainings.** You are needed there. You will find great strength, increased courage and invaluable insight as you fight alongside others who are fighting the good fight just like you. Talk about sticking it to the enemy!! There is nothing he hates more than when you come out of isolation because his power over you is decreased (www.lifechangingservices.org/motherswhoknow).

- **Listen to other mothers figuring things out and sharing their journey.** When you are cleaning the bathroom, doing the dishes, in the shower, or driving, listen to previous class recordings from *Mothers Who Know*.

(Note: Class recordings can be found on the *Mothers Who Know* website under the "Class Recordings" tabs. We recommend you listen to classes with Maurice Harker, CMHC, or Mindy Lundgreen, LCSW, first, and then to others you are interested in. Dads also find great strength and insight in listening to the recordings presented by Maurice Harker.)

"I remember hearing some things in Mothers Who Know that other moms were doing that worked so well for them. I was so excited to try them with my son. None of them worked! I was so upset! Slowly I realized that MY son was not their son, and I knew my son best. So, I tried something else a little different. And it worked great! For a while...until it didn't. I finally learned that I could adapt. As my son changed with the program, and as he got older, I could also change the things we did. If something we were doing wasn't working like it had before, we could change it. And the biggest thing I learned was that it was best to just ask my son how I could help him and support him, in the best way for him. I asked him to be specific and tell me what he thought would be the most helpful to him. Now that was eye-opening! His ideas were very different than mine, but as we implemented them and we were both able to work together, he felt supported, and I fulfilled my need to be involved in his recovery." (A Warrior Mother Who Knows)

#8 - Be an Atmosphere Angel™
YOU can change the tide of battle!

As women, we know we are not the Savior in this war, our children have a Savior, even Jesus Christ. We are the atmosphere angels who can change the very tide of the battle. We know where our power and strength come from. We are safe, strong, peaceful and protective warriors. This is one tough battle for the fighter and the mother of the fighter. Each of us has a battlefield and the enemy of our peace and freedom is very personal about how he attacks. At times our loved ones are dominating their battles and even having obvious improvements in their skills. At other times it will seem they have forgotten how to fight or may be losing the will to fight and win.

I am so thankful for the Savior for this very reason. Because of Him we never lose!! There is always another battle to fight, another day to try, another opportunity to stand up, look up and reach towards Him. There is never a point when He says, "Sorry, you are just too broken. I've been giving you chance after chance and now you are on your own." He understands our battles better than we do. He gave *all* in his fight to stand for our truth and freedom, so we, in our weakness can just keep standing...or trying to...over and over. The victory is literally not in winning 100% of the time, but in never giving up in the fight to win. We do this as we believe in the sacrifice Christ made for us and trust in His promises.

I am the
"ATMOSPHERE ANGEL"
darkness fears...

If you feel scared, afraid, overwhelmed or just plain tired—that is normal. The process is arduous and takes so much faith and tons of personal effort to stay in a believing place. You are an incredibly loving mother full of determined, committed efforts to love and care for your son or daughter like no one else on this earth can right now. Your mother heart is magic for your child in this battle, as is your faith in them and your faith in the Savior. You are literally an atmosphere angel.

You have the ability to speak with love and boldness. Satan wants you to be afraid to speak by whispering, "You will only make things worse." But you know how to enhance the atmosphere of any situation in a nurturing and positive way as you testify of He who is mighty to save! Extend just the right amount of timely affection, perform acts of thoughtful service, express unconditional love, reaffirm your confidence and appreciation for your child's desire to be courageous in battle. Your words, prayers, service, love and expressions can change the very tide (atmosphere) of battle.

It makes me wonder in awe how mothers can carry all we do, face all we face, think about all we think about and not lose our minds? When you consider our workloads - how do we have the strength to get up and face more each day? Why don't we just give up, quit, or just fire everyone and everything? It's too much, right??

There is only one answer to these questions: Christ's loving Atonement.

Through Him, we continue to stand when our knees want to give out and our hearts are in so much pain it seems they will stop beating. Because of Him we can carry loads we feel too inadequate and weak to handle. By His grace, we are able to do more than we can on our own. Through the Spirit we can find the answers we seek "line upon line, precept upon precept" (2 Nephi 28:30).

We are women, mothers, and Heavenly Father's daughters standing, waiting, praying, showing up again, loving still and believing when no one else will. You don't have to be good at it, look pretty doing it, or even know how. You can be broken and do amazing/miraculous things in a very broken way because *you are never alone.*

"The day I reached out to the Mothers Who Know group leader was one of the hardest days in my life. I was still trying to come to grips with _____, I just wanted to run away and hide. I had FAILED!! I contacted Karen (the group leader) because I discovered that this group was one of the free groups offered. I was soooo overwhelmed. I thought I had nothing to lose by attending the mother's group since it was free - it was at least a place to start.

When I said this program has been life changing, I meant it. I think for too long I was just going through life checking the boxes, not really giving anyone or anything the attention it needed. Basically, I was living in my own down and out place wondering if my prayers were just bouncing back. I stayed there not knowing how to jumpstart myself or how to help others beyond the basics. The seminary checklist of prayers, scriptures, church and Family Home Evening was getting checked off, but not with full heart and obviously not empowering me.

It was a class that Karen gave to the mothers' group about prayer that really turned on a switch for me and I took the challenge to really talk to my Heavenly Father. I think that's the moment He was waiting for because suddenly there was light back into my world and, for the first time in a long while, it stayed, unlike the train in the tunnel light...I was ready.

So, what have I learned since then that makes a difference?

- *Prayers are answered! The morning after the class on prayer I knelt and prayed. I told Heavenly Father I was done. Life was getting too hard. __'s health was in a bad spot, work was awful for both of us and I was just plain scared. I told Him (notice told) that I was getting more than I could bear and needed a break. It was a very long and tearful prayer. Shortly after, __ got the complete, out of the blue call for this new job. It wasn't by far my first prayer about any of those trials, but it was more heartfelt and faith-filled than before AND it was answered :-)*
- *Satan is more than just the bad guy, he is the super bad guy and he gets in my head. Instead of letting him get in there and stay I've learned my patterns, I've learned my signs and I'm better equipped to say, "nope not now, I don't have time for that" and can kick the stinkin' thinkin' that's in my head. But I had to learn to see how he was using me and getting to me. And I had to see it was him and not just me beating myself up.*
- *When I am in control of myself and see myself aware of Satan's attacks, I can be more in tune to help point them out (in a positive light) to those in my family. That has been huge!! Instead of wondering why a child is acting a certain way or doing something, I have been more in tune to know that they are having a "chemical spill" moment and work with them using the Spirit instead of enticing Satan to bring it on even more. It was a breakthrough to see that Satan and his minions are the root of so many things.*
- *I've learned that not only does Satan want me, he wants my Priesthood holders. He wants me to be down and out so that I can't support them.*

- *I think one of the best things I have learned is that I am not the Savior for my husband or my boys. I am their support and their cheerleader, but they need the Savior to get through these daily battles. Just like the armies of Helaman, their moms were not on the battlefield fighting with them, but they knew their moms had testimonies and had taught them how to rely on their own faith.*

- *I've learned how real this fight is. I've learned that what my family dealt with (and is still dealing with) is minor compared to what pornography is doing to others...it is so real and so bad. It makes me want to get out of bed with boxing gloves on to make sure we keep things in check.*

- *I can see the hand of the Lord in our getting to this point. When I started going to the temple last summer on a weekly basis, it was because of a prompting. I truly woke up and said, I need the temple. I was stumped as to why I couldn't get __ to come with me as I made it a habit, it seemed so odd. I asked my parents for help and asked for prayers to help me. After a couple of weeks, I knew something was up and I was scared. Yet, it seemed each week in the temple I was given a tool that got me closer to finding out why. Words were put in my mouth to say. I remember asking him, 'Why now? Why are you coming to me now?' That night, I thought that was an odd question, but in hindsight I can see how it all came together and how the Holy Ghost steered it. Satan may mess with us, but Heavenly Father will win, if we use the tools to our benefit...I'm so glad I listened.*

I don't think I have ever felt a drive like I do towards this program. I know what it did for me and what it is doing for my family. I've never seen anything change hearts so quickly.

I haven't changed the world, and I haven't changed everything with our situation, but I know I am on a path bringing me closer to the Savior than I have ever been before. I can feel and see progress. The fight is real and I will keep fighting it." (A courageous Warrior Mother)

#9 - Stay by the Tree
Stay out of your child's battle.

I remember the day I was reading about Lehi's dream in 1 Nephi 8. I had read about this dream many times and remember from my youth days the adages to always "hold to the rod," "hold tight to the iron rod," "never let go of the rod," "the iron rod is the word of God," etc. But this time, as I was in a different stage of life and pondering things I could do as a mother to help my family, I noticed something interesting about this dream, something I had never noticed before - Lehi never leaves the Tree of Life once he arrives!

After traveling in darkness for many hours, Lehi begins to pray and ask the Lord for mercy. Then, after praying, he sees a large field, and at the end a tree with amazing white fruit. Lehi goes to the tree and partakes of the fruit, which he describes as something better than anything he has ever tasted before. After eating of this fruit, he is filled with great joy and wants his family to also have some of this fruit and feel this immense joy. But instead of leaving the tree to go and get his family, he calls to them and tells them each how to get to where he is. He never leaves the safety of the tree!

STAY
by the tree

BECKON
from the tree

Some of his family members make it to the tree and are able to enjoy this fruit also. However, some of his sons would not come to him, they would not choose to enjoy the happiness he was offering. Lehi even sees many of his descendants moving toward the tree with varying degrees of success, many wandering off and getting lost. But Lehi never stops encouraging them, he never stops calling to them and he never leaves. He has found the safety of the Savior and the gospel and the Atonement, and he stays right there next to it all - always hoping his family will choose to join him.

This is when the Spirit was able to teach me, I have to **STAY BY THE TREE**! There is safety and peace there. I must always beckon from the tree. We are always more appealing and influential to those we love and support when we are speaking in the spirit - when we partake at the tree.

In *Mothers Who Know*, we have adopted this ideal to "Stay by the Tree" as our motto. Partake of what the Savior and His Atonement have to offer you in all seasons of life, but especially when facing the challenging storms of life. It becomes a necessity to truly believe in the enabling power of Christ's grace. When in a storm, find shelter, don't panic/keep calm/maintain the spirit and don't forget to eat and drink while you hold on until rescue comes. It is critical to know how Satan tricks you into leaving the tree so he can convince you to get in your child's battle and start becoming weak from the lack of rejuvenating fruit and living water. Inspiring, influential parents know how to *stay by the tree* and how to crush the enemy when he tries to convince them otherwise. No matter what your loved one is doing, stay by the tree. Satan will try over and over again to convince you to leave the tree and run to your loved one to save them; he will even say you are being selfish or rude for not rescuing them. We are smarter than that! Staying by the tree is the most powerful thing we can do for ourselves and for our loved ones who are in this fight. (for the full story, read 1 Nephi chapters 8 and 15).

Who is She?

Who is she, who stays by the Tree?
Amidst battle and strife; the realness of life?
Who holds to the rod, through choices and fog,
Regardless of who holds on with her?
Who plants her feet, leaning into the storm
And beckons from right where she stands?
Who partakes of His love, healed only by One?
The Savior, also, of her little one.
Who is she? Who stands firm by the tree?
Wise to the darkness who seeks her?
Who is she?
The woman is me.

I am a woman who Stays by the Tree.
-A Mother

"Stay by the Tree"
A *Mothers Who Know* original painting
by Judy Cooley
Sold as a fundraiser for our *Mothers Who Know* services.
To order: www.altusfineart.com/stay-by-the-tree/

(Artwork used with permission.)

I am a Mother Who Knows
by Karen Broadhead

I stay by the tree.
Continually holding to the word of God,
I will not be detoured from my divine purpose;
I am a sacred weapon of hope, faith and endless works,
Designed to inspire and love, I can change the very tide of battle.

I beckon from the tree.
Courageously testifying of Christ's power,
I will stand strong and be not moved as I wait upon the Lord.
I am the atmosphere angel darkness fears; I'm awake to deceptions,
Supporting my Savior in His Great Cause of Freedom; I rely upon His arm.

I partake at the tree.
Sanctified through the sweetest, most desirable love,
I will not fear but have power in a sound mind and joy in my soul.
Knowing my identity, empowered by His grace, I am more than enough.
I am a covenant warrior for Jesus Christ, I know what delicious is; I will not be distracted.

There is Hope

Mothers Who Know was created because 10 years ago I was deep in Momma Trauma realizing I had a son in the bonds of addiction to pornography. He was such a noble, amazing young man and I had no idea what to do in that place. I thought I had checked all the right boxes to avoid something like that! I soon realized I didn't understand the science of addiction, I didn't understand that it takes people a long time to heal from addictions, I didn't understand the spiritual side of waiting on the Lord and I didn't understand what my role was as a mother. I felt really isolated and alone.

It was when I learned the life-saving principles I have taught here, that I recognized my life was changing. Today I have so much more personal confidence and peace and I desperately want other mothers to feel the same. In my journey, I learned it wasn't about checking boxes. It was about my heart, it was about being a covenant keeper, it was about who Heavenly Father knew I needed to become and it was about what I needed to learn about mothering a child in a place where I didn't know the answers. I think we all mother children in those places. Whether they are in addiction or in any other things we face as mothers, nobody hands us the answers. The Lord wants us to rely on Him. What I have recognized is nobody knows what they are doing. No one knows how to handle something they haven't done before.

As *Mothers Who Know* we meet online weekly to discuss ways we can strengthen ourselves against the adversary, protect and defend our families and find healing as we strive to access the Light of the World, Jesus Christ.

Jesus Christ taught, *"Blessed are they that mourn: for they shall be comforted"* (Matthew 5:4). A mother's heart can be the first to freely give and the fiercest in a fight for the safety, honor and success of her child. But the truth is, we are at war against an enemy who relentlessly seeks to destroy our families. As mothers in these latter days, despite our desires and vigilance, people we love and fight for can sustain serious wounds. We can find ourselves standing in shock and confusion on a path that doesn't seem to align with our intended celestial course for our family. As we mourn our losses, we can feel isolated, betrayed and full of fear and shame. Perhaps in our darkest place, we believe the deceiving fog of Satan's lies that we are a disappointment to God and we don't deserve His Help.

I am honored to testify, on behalf of thousands of "Mothers Who Know," that **Jesus Christ is the reason for our healing**. It is because of His compassion that we are filled with His light. We can absolutely heal from our own Momma Trauma and find peace through Him.

(To hear mothers share their healing experience, please listen to our 2017 *Light the World* Podcast: http://bit.ly/motherswhoknow)

Mothers Healing
(names withheld to protect privacy)

"When we first discovered my son had a problem with pornography I was stunned. I was overwhelmed and felt so much guilt. I am his mother. I am supposed to protect him from these things. If I had done a better job, then this wouldn't have happened. If I had been more observant...If I had locked down the internet.... I had a million "If I had's..." running through my head, and I felt responsible. I was drowning in feelings of despair and anxiety. I knew I didn't have the knowledge or resources to deal with it. I downloaded _Like Dragons Did They Fight_, [www.lifechangingservices.org/freebook] and read it before we even had his intake appointment. It gave me a game plan and helped me to understand the program, the lingo they use, and how they would help my son. After we met with his clinician and he was in the program, I felt some relief, but I was still consumed with guilt and anxiety for his future. When they sent me the information for the parent resources, I drank it all in. I listened to the parent trainings, watched the orientation video, started listening to the Warrior Mothers Who Know recordings, and joined the Facebook group.

These resources have helped me so much. I feel such a sense of peace when I am involved in them. Sometimes with the busy summer, I wouldn't listen to the recordings as much (I haven't gotten up the nerve to join live yet - I'm a little camera shy) and I could feel my anxiety levels rise. When I listen to other mothers talk about their struggles, I realize I am not alone. When I hear generals talk about their success stories, it gives me hope. When I hear Maurice & Karen answer questions about how the program works, it helps me to understand how Satan works in our lives and how to fight my own battles. Using these resources has helped me to help my son. I realized he needs me to be his mom, not his clinician. I know I could easily have drowned in sorrow and guilt. I am so grateful these resources exist, they have given me peace and hope in the power of the Savior and His Atonement and the power we have to change and fight our battles." (A new Warrior Mother)

"First, I want to say how thankful I am for the Sons of Helaman program and for the amazing resource of the Mothers Who Know website (www.lifechangingservices.org/motherswhoknow)! When our family first learned that our son had the addiction problem with Mr. P and M [pornography and masturbation], we were, of course, completely devastated.

Interestingly enough, I had seen a post on Facebook from a friend about the program almost a year before, and so I was able to go back and find that information for our son and family to utilize.

First and foremost, I downloaded the free E-book Like Dragons Did They Fight for our son, myself and husband to read. Our son could not believe how accurate the information was and also relevant to what he had been trying to battle on his own (unsuccessfully) for almost a year. He was so relieved to find something he felt could finally help him! So were his Dad and I!

I want to tell anyone (mothers especially) who is reading this, that both my husband and I have had to really trust in the program and the process. We were in a very dark place and felt completely helpless. We had to have FAITH in the Savior and the enabling power of the Atonement. With a lot of prayer, scripture study, temple attendance, discussion and communication between us all, we have been able to begin the baby steps of healing." (A Warrior Mother)

"I purchased the book Like Dragons Did They Fight for my husband and I and also one for our son to read. After a few days my husband and I talked to our son and he agreed to begin the program. I also began to utilize all the information on the Mothers Who Know website under "Suggestions for Parents." I found the four recorded Parent Training Recordings to be incredibly helpful for me to begin healing. I found great peace as I listened to Karen present to parents that were going through what I was. I can't tell you how many times I have listened to her over the last 4 months. I also began listening to the Tuesday at 10:30 a.m. trainings and began to

*review the previous recorded classes and General's Panel as well –
AWESOME!*

*I also purchased and read <u>Putting on the Armor of God</u>, by
Steven A. Cramer, to read along with our son. I am now on my
second read of that book and have found it to be an incredible
resource for me as I study. I really think I have been asleep to this
WAR we are in. Not anymore. I am a powerful atmosphere angel for
my family and will not let Satan or his minions manipulate me
anymore.*

*About 6 weeks ago, our son had a setback and through a
back door in his email accessed some pornography. We had thought
we had everything locked down, but because of this, we decided to
consult with More Safe Mark. This was the BEST decision!!! Mark
came to our home and listened to us, then made recommendations
that have helped us immensely. Now we can all sleep well (and just
function throughout the day) knowing that our family is protected.
Our son especially was so thankful to know that he could begin to
use the internet again and be safe and protected.*

*I have learned so much in such a short amount of time, and
have awareness like I have never had before in my life, of the enemy
- Satan, and what he is trying to do to my family. Now I have the
tools to fight as well. It's with this program and the many resources
from the Mothers Who Know website, that I have gained this
confidence and have started to heal. My relationship with our son
has increased so much. We really talk and have deep discussions,
and I can be a real support for him. I look forward to the evenings
when we visit about his day and listen with awe as he tells me of the
battles he fights and wins each day! Some days are very hard, and
setbacks happen, but this program is saving our son!*

*Mothers, do not give up on your sweet sons! LOVE them,
pray for them to remember who they are. Have incredible patience
for them. Do not stop your own healing either. Find what helps you
most and keep moving forward. It gets easier one day at a time.
Most of all...love your son and know that he can WIN by learning
the tools to help protect him and his future family. He can go on to
live a successful, productive life – confident, happy and emotionally
healthy.*

*Thank you, Karen, for all that you do each and every day!
You are a ROCK STAR and I hope to be able to meet you in person
someday.*

As you say: Together in the Fight!" (A Warrior Mom)

My Story of Gratitude

After eight years of watching my son struggle with an addiction to masturbation and pornography, he finally received his mission call. His departure date was pushed back twice due to lost battles. When he got out into the field, I could tell from his letters, efforts and diligence he was there to stay and stay strong. I thought my heart would burst with gratitude; we had finally arrived at recovery.

When he returned home from his honorable two-year mission I thought he was good to go. The shock and heartbreak I had when he started losing battles devastated me. The fear of going back to all those years of fighting this battle with my noble son terrified me. Now as a man, he needed to be worthy to do needful man things like choose a career, date for the purpose of marriage, etc. Fortunately, because of his pre-mission training in Sons of Helaman, coupled with all he had gained from his mission and his quick return back in a Sons of Helaman group for support, he quickly got his warrior tools back into swing with an even greater spirit. He headed to college. He met a beautiful woman and was soon married. I thought my heart would burst with grateful happiness.

Then I received a phone call in the dark early morning hours the day after my son's first child was born. He knew my daily schedule started early and I would be awake. He whispered as not to wake his sleeping wife. He had picked his tiny daughter up out of her little hospital crib so her squeaking noises wouldn't wake his exhausted wife. He brought his baby daughter to lay in his arms as he lay on his bed in their dark hospital room. He said he wanted to share something special with me and proceeded to say something like this, 'Mom, I just have to share with you how special this is to be here in this room and now have two of Heavenly Father's daughters to care for and protect. I feel so honored and such a great responsibility to them and to Heavenly Father. But the thing I feel, that I knew you would appreciate, is that as I lay here with my tiny, now sleeping daughter and my wife sleeping there in her bed, I am overcome with the gratitude I'm feeling as I consider I am completely worthy and there is nothing unclean inside me.' We both shed some tears and he expressed his confidence and desire to preside, provide and protect his girls (something I knew was drilled into him in his Sons of Helaman groups) and expressed his belief in his ability to do it in the way he would make me and God proud. That was a moment like no other I have experienced with my son before or since. My heart was so full of gratitude for my good son and for the recovery he was able to find with the support and training of this program. I was grateful for the safety he made me feel. Most of all, I was full of gratitude for a Savior whom I loved with all my heart, for healing both my son and me and allowing me this tender, beautiful moment that was a great victory and balm to my mother heart. (Karen)

For more information on *Mothers Who Know* or any of the programs offered at Life Changing Services, please visit www.lifechangingservices.org or call us at 877-HERO-877. You can also schedule a free one on one visit with Karen via an online zoom format by going to www.lifechangingservices.youcanbook.me/.

(Note: you do not need to have a child in a Life Changing Services program to participate in *Mothers Who Know*. These groups are open and available to ALL women who want to better educate themselves to fight against the adversary, stand strong in the face of adversity, and strengthen their families).

5 SCRIPTURES
Mothers
Need to Hear
(Especially Hurting Ones)

1. For Strength – Helaman 5:12

"And now, my **daughters***, remember, remember that it is upon the rock of our Redeemer, who is Christ, the Son of God, that ye must build your foundation; that when the devil shall send forth his mighty winds, yea, his shafts in the whirlwind, yea, when all his hail and his mighty storm shall beat upon you, it shall have no power over you to drag you down to the gulf of misery and endless wo, because of the rock upon which you are built, which is a sure foundation, a foundation whereon if men build they cannot fail."*

Strong as a rock- Satan has no power over you.

2. For Power – D&C 128:22

*"***Sisters***, shall we not go on in so great a cause? Go forward and not backward. Courage,* **sisters***; and on, on to the victory! Let your hearts rejoice and be exceedingly glad..."*

YOU MATTER - YOUR EFFORTS MEAN MIRACLES!

3. For Hope – 2 Timothy 1:7

"For God hath not given us the spirit of fear; but of power, and of love, and of a sound mind."

Fear is from the enemy. Love and power are from God!

4. For Cheerfulness– D&C 123:17

"Therefore, dearly beloved **sisters***, let us cheerfully do all things that lie in our power, and then may we stand still, with the utmost assurance, to see the salvation of God, and for his arm to be revealed."*

Trust in the arm of the Lord to be cheerful.

5. For Courage – Joshua 1:9

"Have not I commanded thee? Be strong and of good courage; be not afraid, neither be thou dismayed; for the Lord thy God is with thee withersoever thou goest."

I am STRONG and COURAGEOUS!
My Savior and Champion is with me.

(If you would like to download a jpg version of this for yourself, go to www.bit.ly/5scripturesformothers)

Appendix

MOM PoWeR Calendar

(Note: The MOM PoWeR calendar is a little different than calendars used in other programs at Life Changing Services. It is less about self-mastery and more about healing Momma Trauma. The way success is defined and tracked is also different.)

"Mothers Who Know" live their life *on purpose* for Christ. They don't let their life live them!

The MOM PoWeR Calendar is a training tool designed to instill within your mind and spirit the power and weapons needed to claim the *"fruit of the Spirit"* (Galatians 5:22-23). It is designed to help you **be a mother who is peaceful, strong and confident in the storms of life**. It is designed to help you protect and defend your family as you guard your testimony and put God's cause first.

We are at war between REMEMBERING and forgetting our divine identity and purpose as women. Our enemy is Satan. He will try every day to misrepresent our truth, make us believe we are less than we are and tell us our performance is tied to our identity. If we only notice what we lack in our efforts and ability, we become vulnerable to Satan's lies about our divine purpose. We are daughters of God! Never underestimate the fear Satan has of you and your abilities to thwart his destructive efforts with those you love.

The overall objective of using your calendar is to assist you in doing things "on purpose" each day and to assist you in noticing things that are going right. The goal is to achieve a "**Purposeful**" (not necessarily perfect) day in each of your 6 actions so you can *"always remember him...[and] always have his Spirit to be with [you]"* (D&C 20:77).

Each Day I Fight to REMEMBER:

My Savior - I will rely upon Him. I have help. I am not alone. Only He can save.

Own My Truth - I protect and defend my divine identity and purpose as a woman. I am the atmosphere angel.

Minister - I serve others to assist God in His work. I am #1 on His support team. I love the cause of Christ and cheering for people I love.

Each Day I Fight to Stay Connected to God:

Pray – I talk to God as if everything depends on Him, then I show up with purpose as if everything depends on me. I know the Lord is patient with me and understands this can be at different levels each day.

Write – I love the Lord and want to hear what He has to say to me. I write to slow down MY will and hear God's. I am sincere, meek and teachable as I invite and allow God to help me find answers.

Read – As I read, I listen carefully and with expectant faith to hear the answers and guidance God has for me and my family. I *"feast upon the words of Christ"* (2 Nephi 32:3) to access more power, stay connected to my truth and discern the tactics of the adversary. I read so *"the words of Christ will tell [me] all things what [I] should do"* (2 Nephi 32:3).

EXAMPLES—MOM PoWeR in Action

Examples of MOM actions: (Pick one to do and track for at least a month).

M (My Savior): Create, add to, or study 3x5 "mini iron rod" cards daily. (These are statements you collect that are powerful to you. They can be favorite scriptures, quotes, memes, etc. They can be actual 3x5 cards or an app on your phone.) Remember Him with music, audio of spiritual text, personal singing, prayer, art or reciting. Study about how He is the only Savior. Notice His help each day and His tender mercies. Write a personal declaration using scriptures, hymns or words of prophets that testify of who the Savior is for you. Do a special act of service each day for

Christ. Memorize Christ-centered documents and statements. Note the lies Satan tells you and refuse them. Choose positive language and thoughts to show your faith. Go outside and stand on a big rock and recite Helaman 5:12.

O (Own my Truth): Say by memory or read out loud your personal declaration. Write down at least 3 things each day that are going right. Work on the TRUTH Tool in your journal. Do a self-care routine. Find one quote or scripture each day that restores your truth and add it to your "my truth" file (from the Truth Tool). Write down the lies you hear in your head and release them (burn, flush, rip or throw away). Do one thing out of your comfort zone each day. Go outside to breathe deep and state your truth. Do something you enjoy. Laugh/cry and write why you matter to God, yourself and your family. Study your patriarchal blessing and note who you are.

M (Minister): Perform an act of service. Reach out to someone in love and let them know they matter. Make a meal for your family. Send a letter or note. Help someone with their chore/job. Declare someone else's truth. Support someone in battle by just expressing your love and belief in them. Talk to a stranger and compliment their efforts. Share the gospel or your testimony. Do family history work. Have a sincere prayer about/for someone. Notice who is on God's support team and nurture those relationships.

Examples of PoWeR actions: (These are constant and are tracked always. They can be enhanced or reduced because life is real - but endeavor to never skip.)

P: Pray to have a meaningful connection with God. Listen each time before you end your prayer. Work on being sincere, open and honest. Use a timer to pray for a certain length of time. Take note of your impressions and thoughts. Pray in a place you can speak out loud and can say the thoughts of your heart. Stay connected to heaven in prayer-thoughts all day. Say prayers of gratitude as you count your blessings. Ask God specifically for those things you desire and hope for. Pray for courage and peace.

W: Write a letter to God every day. You can also write to your future or past self, a loved one (present, passed on or yet to be born) or your spouse. You can write letters to yourself in the spirit as if from God. Write about your patriarchal blessing, your testimony about gospel topics or your divine truth (my identity and/or purpose.) Write about things that are going right and express gratitude. Write about things you are learning in your reading/study and prayers to show the Lord you are listening and value His council. Write with intent to receive revelation for you and your loved ones.

R: Read until you find something that touches your heart or teaches you something. Read your "mini iron-rod cards" (see "M" My Savior above), the scriptures, conference talks, devotionals, church magazines, etc. Read to be filled with your truth and the love of God. Read to build spiritual discernment.

I AM A MOTHER WHO KNOWS! DAILY, I REMEMBER WHY I FIGHT AND WHY I NEVER GIVE UP - **ON PURPOSE**!

Tips for Success:

- Realize you are already doing SO MANY THINGS right!
- Understand this is not a tool to show you all the things you need to improve upon. (Warning: Satan will often try to tell you it is a failure tracker.)
- Celebrate with gratitude and joy what you *are* doing. Notice all the good things you do each day.
- Start where you're at. You may just start with PWR actions (even *one* power action) until you feel some momentum.
- Change your MOM actions after you notice you have consistent wins, on purpose, over a period of time, or feel led by the Spirit.
- Be alert to Satan's lies: "I don't feel like it." "I can do it later." "I don't need to set an alarm or write that down; I can remember it." "It won't matter if I miss just this once." "You work so hard and you are too tired." "You're too upset and sad...just give up today." "You already missed an action for today...the rest don't matter." When you are ambushed with these thoughts, claim your power by doing the action anyway. It doesn't have to be pretty or perfect.
- If your calendar is blank for a while, don't quit...God knows the desires of your heart and cares about your pain. He is not disappointed in you. He only loves you and is standing by to assist. Just start again...wherever you are.
- Goals can be adjusted to make your calendar work for YOU...You don't work for your calendar.
- Set up a contingency plan ahead of time if you know you will be out of your usual routine, for example: vacation days, sick day, kids home from school, special events, holidays, etc. Set yourself up to succeed.
- Get involved with a team and be accountable.
- Ask the Lord to help you and tell Him what you hope to accomplish.
- **Everything you do is a win**; notice it as such.
- Notice patterns of negative thoughts and emotions and evaluate how Satan is distracting or deceiving you. Notice what triggers your moods.
- Practice strategies to change negative thoughts and feelings. Do something on purpose with your body: clean out a drawer/desk, walk around the block or your office, dance to a favorite song, fold a load of laundry, push your child on the swing, shake the rugs,

rock a baby, call a friend, read to a child, sing to the radio, etc. Use the TRUTH Tool.

➢ If you miss a day or even a week on your PWR actions, but you still show up *on purpose* to start again, it's a double win! God asks us to keep trying, to keep believing, to keep trusting in Him. Every effort we make to follow Him is a win! In small ways or big ways, He cheers our efforts.

➢ Keep your calendar where you can see it at all times for accountability and as a reminder.

➢ Recognize *with purpose* that your calendar is an *offensive* weapon you use to reclaim your power and show Satan he is messing with the wrong mom. Your actions are also used as *defensive* weapons to fight your way back to the fruit of the Spirit, to the love of God and to "The Tree".

➢ Reach out for assistance to the *Mothers Who Know* team if you have questions, would like help setting up your actions, need an objective view to help you evaluate your progress truthfully without Satan's lies, need another atmosphere angel to relate to or cheer for you or just want to say hello. Email us at wearemotherswhoknow@gmail.com. We can't wait to hear from you! ☺

To download a full-page version of the MOM PoWeR Calendar, go to www.bit.ly/MOMPWR (tip: use all caps when typing MOMPWR into your browser).

MOM PoWeR Calendar

Day:			Day:			Day:			Day:			Day:			Day:			Day:		
M	O	M	M	O	M	M	O	M	M	O	M	M	O	M	M	O	M	M	O	M
P	W	R	P	W	R	P	W	R	P	W	R	P	W	R	P	W	R	P	W	R
Day:			Day:			Day:			Day:			Day:			Day:			Day:		
M	O	M	M	O	M	M	O	M	M	O	M	M	O	M	M	O	M	M	O	M
P	W	R	P	W	R	P	W	R	P	W	R	P	W	R	P	W	R	P	W	R
Day:			Day:			Day:			Day:			Day:			Day:			Day:		
M	O	M	M	O	M	M	O	M	M	O	M	M	O	M	M	O	M	M	O	M
P	W	R	P	W	R	P	W	R	P	W	R	P	W	R	P	W	R	P	W	R
Day:			Day:			Day:			Day:			Day:			Day:			Day:		
M	O	M	M	O	M	M	O	M	M	O	M	M	O	M	M	O	M	M	O	M
P	W	R	P	W	R	P	W	R	P	W	R	P	W	R	P	W	R	P	W	R

M = My Savior:	I will rely upon Him. I have help. I am not alone. Only He can save.
O = Own My Truth:	I protect and defend my divine identity and purpose as a woman. I am the atmosphere angel.
M = Minister:	I serve others to assist God in His work. I am #1 on His support team. I love the cause of Christ and cheering for people I love.
P = Prayer:	I talk to God as if everything depends on Him, then I show up with purpose as if everything depends on me. I know the Lord is patient with me and understands this can be at different levels each day.
W= Write:	I love the Lord and want to hear what He has to say to me. I write to slow down MY will and hear God's. I am sincere, meek and teachable as I invite and allow God to help me find answers.
R = Read:	As I read, I listen carefully and with expectant faith to hear the answers and guidance God has for me and my family. I *"feast upon the words of Christ"* (2 Nephi 32:3) to access more power, stay connected to my truth and discern the tactics of the adversary. I read so *"the words of Christ will tell [me] all things what [I] should do"* (2 Nephi 32:3).

81

About the Author

Upon learning one of her noble sons had become ensnared in the bonds of pornography addiction, Karen L. Broadhead felt powerless and afraid in her search for healing resources for her son. Inspired by the impact the Sons of Helaman program had on her son's life, she asked Maurice Harker, the director at Life Changing Services if she could start a support program for parents struggling to support their sons and daughters in addiction. Karen set out to build what is now called *Mothers Who Know*. As Founder & Director of the *Mothers Who Know* support program, her knowledge and influence for hope have grown. Karen now serves not only her son and her family but also many others. This online support group and free weekly online training program now serves women all over the country.

Karen is a certified LCS Life Coach. She specializes in serving women and families in pain or trauma. She has taught hundreds of students as an Eternal Warriors Mentor with Life Changing Services and has over 400 hours of class recordings available for free download on her *Mothers Who Know* blog. She also serves as the Parent Support Specialist within the Sons of Helaman and Daughters of Light therapeutic recovery programs of Life Changing Services. She has served as a board member on the Utah Coalition Against Pornography and currently serves on the Reach 10 Advisory Board.

Momma Trauma: Now What? is Karen's first book. It is a compilation of the principles and training she has developed and shared as a Life Coach, Eternal Warriors Mentor, Parent Support Specialist, *Mothers Who Know* director and Warrior Mother over the past 10 years. Her purpose is to share hope and increase light for women and families. Karen has a bachelor's degree in Recreational Therapy from Brigham Young University.

Karen L. Broadhead is a wife, mother, grandmother, daughter, sister, friend and member of The Church of Jesus Christ of Latter-day Saints. Karen and her husband, Kent, have five children, nine grandchildren and live in the beautiful mountains of Utah. Karen loves being a mother and wife and is committed to sharing a message of hope and happiness because she knows "our mess can become our message" even our miracle.

Karen's Personal Declaration: *"I am a fearless warrior for Jesus Christ. I stand strong for His great cause of truth and freedom. I am connected with the Savior at all times, committed to fulfill the plan for my life that we make together. I am filled with the light of Jesus Christ and stand proudly in my own truth."*

If you have a specific concern or question, you can email Karen at wearemotherswhoknow@gmail.com.

To schedule a free 30-minute one-on-one meeting with Karen: www.lifechangingservices.youcanbook.me/.